MAPPING PERCEPTION

Proboscis
London

First published in 2002 by Proboscis,
2 Ormonde Mansions, 100A Southampton Row,
London WC1B 4BJ, United Kingdom,
www.proboscis.org.uk

Book edited by Giles Lane & Katrina Jungnickel
with Mark Lythgoe
Designed by Allyson Waller
Printed by Geoff Neal Litho
BarbieXR3i typeface by Jason Rainbird

CD-ROM edited by Alice Angus
Designed & programmed by Nima Falatoori, NMoDesign

Thanks to the contributors:
Eden Kötting, Toby McMillan, Janna Levin, Professor
Richard Gregory, Professor David Gadian, Craig Bennett,
Phillip Chance, Kling Chong, Ian Glass, Chloe Hutton,
Melissa Parisi, David Thomas and Bryony Whiting.

ISBN: 1 901540 21 9

British Library cataloguing-in-publication data: a catalogue
record for this book is available at the British Library.

This publication has been made possible through the
generous support of: Sciart Consortium (Production Award
Winner 2000), Film Council (National Lottery Award),
London Production Fund, Calouste Gulbenkian Foundation
& South East Arts.

www.mappingperception.org.uk

Introduction – Giles Lane & Katrina Jungnickel

*Science is not a heartless pursuit of objective information...
it is a creative human activity, its geniuses acting more as
artists than as information processors.*
Stephen Jay Gould, *Ever Since Darwin*

Scientists and artists share an unquenchable curiosity
and desire to question the world in which we live.
Their methods, processes and outcomes may be worlds
apart but their journeys can intertwine in united
voyages of discovery. *Mapping Perception* is just such
an experimental entanglement – the sum of four years
of collaborative thinking, arguing, discussing, sharing and
creating, born of a shared passion, a common interest –
perception.

A Brief History

Mapping Perception is a unique collaborative project
commissioned by Proboscis, a practitioner-led
cultural organisation which is dedicated to creating
and commissioning work which cuts across social,
cultural and professional divides.

Mapping Perception was conceived and initiated by
Giles in late 1997 who brought together Andrew, a
filmmaker, and Mark, a neurophysiologist at the Institute
of Child Health. Giles had previously commissioned
independent work from both Andrew and Mark for
issue 2 of COIL journal of the moving image published
by Proboscis in 1995. Mark was commissioned for his
first science-art project *Images of the Mind* (with Helen
Sear) and Andrew presented *Twit Gone Drank*, a text
and image piece.

Andrew, Giles and Mark all share a desire to bridge
their different cultural disciplines and forge a new
language to question human perception and to
challenge the membrane that separates the normal
and the abnormal. From this entanglement many
outcomes have resulted: a film (subtitled 'an
experimental documentary describing a scientific
love poem'), an installation, a book and a CD-ROM
as well as a life experience that will not disappear
quickly.

The first iteration of the project was a short-listed
proposal for the 1998 Sciart scheme then run by the
Wellcome Trust. This interest in the basic ideas of the
collaboration led Giles and Andrew to re-think and
re-work the outcomes during 1998 before meeting up
with Mark in the Autumn. The project's scope expanded
considerably during this time, eventually arriving at the
outcomes we see today.

From the Autumn of 1998 Andrew, Giles and Mark
began to meet regularly and from there the project
began to take off. These meetings and discussions
thrashed out the intellectual and aesthetic framework
for the project which Mark and Giles then presented at
a science-art seminar held at Imperial College London
in June 1999.

A few months later, in September, the first of the
funders to commit to the project was the London
Production Fund (administered by the London Film
& Video Development Agency). They were followed
in February 2000 by South East Arts, and then by the
Sciart Consortium's Production Award in April 2000.
The Film Council awarded the project National Lottery
Funding in July 2000, and the Calouste Gulbenkian
Foundation awarded a special grant to conduct further
research in February 2001. Many discussions were
held between 1998 and 2000 with the Edinburgh
International Film Festival who were keen to premiere

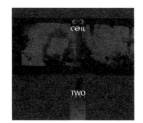
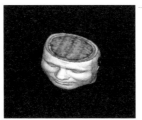

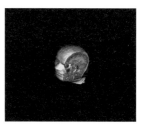

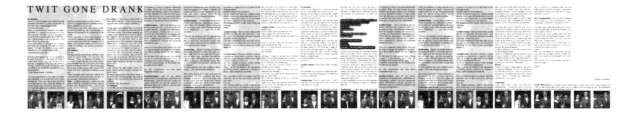

both the film and the installation, even going so far as to select a venue for the installation.

The long period of development on *Mapping Perception* thus moved into a production phase in Summer 2000, albeit with a hiatus when Andrew snuck off to shoot his feature film *This Filthy Earth*, which received financial backing just as *Mapping Perception* gathered momentum.

An Outline
Mapping Perception examines the limits of human perception through an investigation of impaired brain function to further understand the mind and body interaction and our relationship with its abnormality. This dual display of what is seen and what courses beneath the surface brings us to the core substance of what we perceive in ourselves and others. It aims to make visible the connections between the scientific and artistic explorations of the human condition, probing the thin membrane between the able and the disabled.

At the heart of the project is Eden, Andrew's daughter. She was born at Guy's Hospital, London, in 1988 with a rare genetic disorder – Joubert Syndrome – causing cerebral vermis hypoplasia and several other neurological complications. Eden thus participates in the project as both a catalyst and a cipher for a more general investigation into how we see the world and perceive difference.

The collaboration aimed to be symbiotic: the different approaches of critical thinking, artistic practice and scientific methodology operating like a series of antagonistic pairs; a duality to which the ironic title hints – between science's belief in the reducibility of human experience to essential physiological elements and the philosophical chimera that is 'perception'. *Mapping Perception* is thus a unique kind of collaboration between a curator, an artist and a scientist: working together they have challenged not only how art and culture benefit from science, but also how science benefits from art and culture. The results are a genuine attempt for the 'Two Cultures' to work together to produce a body of work that is both art and a product of scientific research, not merely that of an artist using the technologies of science, nor a scientist making use of aesthetic images to describe scientific techniques. It sets out to rethink attitudes and to position artistic and scientific practices at the leading edge of social debate on perceptions of disability.

The project took its initial inspiration from Eden's condition, but it has been the implications of disability on the senses and the exploration of perception itself, that the collaborators' discussions have opened up, "Why do we see only in visible light" and, "What would world look like if we could sense polarised light instead of visible?" It is our senses that guide us and it has been the interpretation of Eden's and our perception, though a mutual language of art and science, which has resulted in this project. The outcomes blend technology, science and personal enquiry to accentuate the charismatic humanism that the dialogue between art and the science exposes.

Contributions

Mapping Perception is the fruit of not only Andrew's, Giles' and Mark's collaboration, but of many other people's contributions. Eden was central to the whole process of creating the work, as was her mother, Leila. Toby McMillan's work on the sound design is fundamental to the overall feel of the project as were Dudley Sutton's, Benji Ming's and Billie Macloed Kötting's performances. We could not have completed such a complex and exhaustive project without the support of Professor David Gadian at the Institute of Child Health and many of Mark's colleagues, including Sally Dowsett, Chloe Hutton, Bryony Whiting, David Thomas, Kling Chong, Katy Price, Melissa Lees, Steve Smith, Wah Poon, Alan Connelly, Alison Rowan, Martin King and Catherine Deville, Robert Surtees, Kate Quine, Robyn Haselfoot, Heather Ducie, Phillip Chance (and colleagues) have also contributed greatly along the way. We are very fortunate to be able to include three texts by Richard Gregory in this volume as a result of his interest and support.

Technical support for the project was crucial and we thank Stephen Connolly, Berkley Cole and Nick Gordon Smith for their continued input. Gary Parker shot additional material at Kent Institute of Art & Design in November 2001, and huge thanks are due to Russell and Jonny Stopford at Remote Films, without whose support we would never have completed the film.

Thanks to Ron Henocq at Café Gallery Projects for exhibiting an installation that had so many unknown elements attached, and to Lizzie Franke, Nicola Pierson and Linda Crooks who worked with us at the Edinburgh Film Festival.

Many others have also contributed in ways too disparate to account for: Ben Woolford and Dan Weldon at Tall Stories Ltd, John Penfold, John Roseveare, Cliff West, Sean Lock, The Joubert Foundation, Michael Clark at the Wellcome Trust Library, Janna Levin, Lucy Shanahan, Kent Institute of Art and Design, David Leister, The Arts Catalyst and Louyre.

Thanks are due to Alice Angus, Katrina Jungnickel and Catherine Williams at Proboscis, and to Nima Falatoori and Allyson Waller for their compelling designs.

Finally we must thank our funders for their vision, commitment and understanding of the exigencies of long term collaborations: Maggie Ellis (London Production Fund), Tim Cornish (South East Arts), Bergit Arends (Sciart Consortium) and Clare Lovett (NESTA), Marie Case (Film Council) and Sian Ede (Calouste Gulbenkian Foundation).

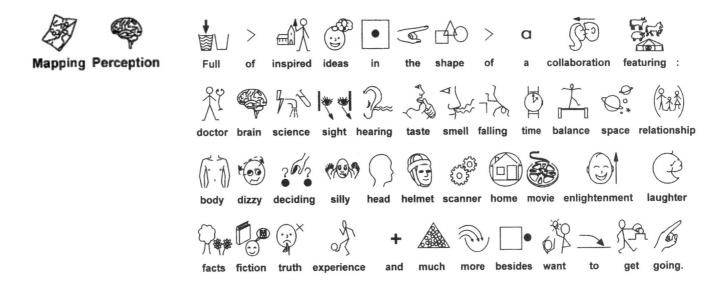

Blurred Vision – a dialogue between Giles Lane & Katrina Jungnickel

Katrina Jungnickel: *Mapping Perception is an amazingly ambitious title for a project.*

Giles Lane: The title stems from when I first commissioned Mark for another project in 1995. At the time certain attitudes in medical research were asserting that, via a single blood sample or image, we could capture our individuality. With the advent of functional magnetic resonance imaging (see Chloe Hutton) we discussed whether this was becoming the new reality. I felt that this was excessively reductivist. The idea of mapping perception itself is mad and that's why it is such a powerful idea. It's an ironic title, because it is absurd to think we could possibly map perception when there are six billion people on the planet, each of whom have a subjective perception of the world. How could you make sense of the way six billion people make sense?

When I brought Andrew and Mark together in 1998, we talked about the theme of how we understand normality and abnormality and how it's driven by perception. I see perception as the subjective use of the human senses to understand and interact with phenomenological existence. It's about how we make sense of and interact with the world in a phenomenological way. And I think it is part of the human condition that we are always trying to develop ways of understanding that are generic, or universal. But the problem is that in the process of attempting to do that, the exception proves the rule. So we constantly make exceptions and then the exceptions lead us down other paths towards new kinds of 'universal' approaches, because none of them will ever suffice.

And the tag for the film is a multi-layered blurring between science and art.

'An experimental documentary describing a scientific love poem', is the subtitle for the film, something we have talked about for a long time. The love poem is clearly from Andrew to Eden, and to a degree from Mark to Eden, because Mark has become part of their broader family as a result of four years of working together. Also they have used scientific analysis of Eden's condition and thought about how science categorises people and categorises illness. A lot of the archive film and sound used in the film is very much a part of this, trying to capture the attitudes of science. The historical framework of medical science we have inherited treats patients and people with illness in a deeply paternalistic way. Attempting to create a piece of work which critiques such paternalism and makes someone who would otherwise be an object of scientific research into a person is truly important.

There is a particularly shocking archive image in the film where a scientist holds up a deformed baby and, later on in the film, a disembodied voice refers to a child as an 'it'. Another voice in the film says: "…it doesn't exactly look like a human being yet. Although its has a heart that beats". This is disturbing because it is a really paternalistic view of society and a judgment of elements that don't fit, that are more complex. It is an important part of the project to question that, to say that the child being held up there is still a human being and that just because they can't communicate with us, doesn't mean they shouldn't have rights. We should be making the effort to communicate with them. That child might have amazing insights, or might be able to perceive things about our world and ourselves that we can't see.

These are the major issues being questioned by the project and we needed to reflect them in a way that reaches beyond the art-going public to the general populace and the science community.

In the original sciart application, Mapping Perception had a 'genuine intent' for the two cultures to work together and produce a new piece of work that was both art and science. Do you think that has happened?

A lot of art is used as a means of articulating complex science in an entertaining way. And a lot of scientists don't understand that art is a serious investigation into the human condition – into experience, memory and love – these things that science in some respects is more or less engaged in exploring. Yet the project demonstrates that scientists and artists can collaborate with different aims and objectives, whilst pursuing similar kinds of questions. The so-called 'two cultures' of C.P. Snow can work together.

After four years or intense collaboration, this project must have had an effect on all of you.

Andrew has been eloquent in his descriptions of how the project has affected him as an artist. He has never worked on this kind of collaborative project over such a long period of time and I think it has changed the way he thinks of himself as an artist. In the first two years of the project he did a lot of research into Joubert Syndrome (which Eden suffers from), which he had not actually done as a parent, because he was so busy coping on a day-to-day basis.

One the most profound things that Mark told me was that he had never directly experienced these conditions as being part of a person before. They were just a collection of signs and symptoms which he investigated to help people. Through Eden he got to know someone in a way that he had never, as a research scientist, got

to know them before. The process of working on the project has stimulated him to question not the scientific methodology, but rather the direction of science and medicine.

In the long term we need to find ways to document how the process has affected Mark as a scientist. Through our discussions Mark has been challenged to think about the implications of the ways in which abnormality was being represented in 2D or 3D images. In order to enhance the ways we perceive Eden's condition, Mark was led to work with programmers in the imaging department to design new 3D imaging algorithms for the data sets being produced from MRI. Following the development of these algorithms, Mark feels that it is these almost imperceptible changes which influence his way of working.

And yet our perception of science is that it is the truth, conducted purely in our best interests.

Exactly. The project also tries to reveal aspects of the social construction of our understandings of science. One of the key issues we need to address as a society is the subjectivity of the topics of scientific endeavour, where it is driven by economic forces influencing scientific institutions. Ultimately the money for research comes from the government, pharmaceutical companies or from medical charities that have specific outcomes in mind, such as answers for particular illnesses or diseases. This makes research contingent upon the consensus of such economic forces which govern the flow of funding: it is mostly top down not bottom up.

The image we have chosen to represent the project – the recreation of Rembrandt's *The Anatomy Lesson of Professor Nicholas Tulp* – questions both science's naïvete and paternalism. Four men look down on a child, it is a male gaze, a very masculine endeavour.

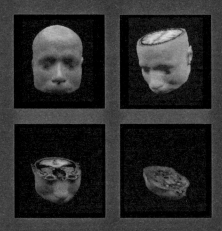

The image harks back to a time when only men were allowed to engage in scientific activity, alluding to the authoritative voice of the scientist as father-figure, all knowing and unassailable in his self-knowledge. It also harks back to the science that looks at people like objects, where the scientist has willingly become devoid of social context and been raised on a pedestal. Around that time in history it was not uncommon for medical professors to lecture their students on dissection from afar, whilst a porter actually cut open the body and handled the innards. We aimed to critically question science's monolithic role in contemporary culture. In the male dominated society that we have inherited, the aspects of masculine cultures that large monolithic institutions like medical science have taken on is clearly not a good thing. I actually see *Mapping Perception* as being, overall, a much more balanced and feminine approach to thinking in a non-hierarchical and non-deterministic way and much more open to difference, which I see as being a more feminine quality in our general makeup as humans.

The project explores so many different ways of looking. We see from the perspectives of 16th century and modern day scientists, through the eyes of a parent and filmmaker, as well as through changing social codes.

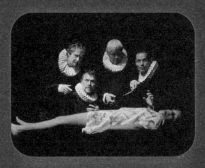

I think it is very important to have many ways of looking. Rather than simplify something to make it understandable, we are trying to indicate the breadth and complexity of daily life for everybody. These issues just can't be boiled down. Because of the nature of the world we live in and the nature of the situation, particularly in the West, we are always trying to make sense of complexity. Other cultures seem to be able to incorporate notions of complexity in general culture without simplifying them. The ciphers they use are simultaneously simple and complex. They don't try to hide complexity, it is simply built into them. It's like the onion skin. You keep peeling it and eventually you peel

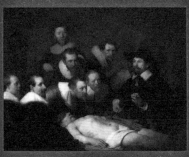

away the layers and layers that create the object itself. There is no centre.

In terms of how I work, layering is extremely important. So many people tend to try to go for grand theories and master narratives that shoe everything in, though it never quite fits. As a result, you get into endless debates because nicely-boxed master narratives compete with each one. Then you have layers and layers of narratives which all have elements of truth or veracity, or degrees in which they are truths to different people at different times in different situations. It was important for this project not to go for a master narrative at all, but to create as many layers as possible. The risk with doing that is that people may not understand or perceive the richness. Because there is so much involved in this project, (the film, installation, book and CD-ROM), we are hoping to inspire people to delve deeply. We hope it will challenge people not to look for the simplified, dumbed down version but to appreciate the complexity on as many levels as they are interested. The project itself does not map perception in any way, it just throws up questions and makes the whole issue more and more problematic.

The film is a very intimate and personal portrayal of Eden through the eyes of her filmmaker father. Yet the whole project is bigger than the film.

The project is very large, and the film has become just one way into it. We didn't just want to make a piece of art. The film, installation, book, website and CD-ROM are about challenging ordinary people to rethink their prejudices about what is normal and what is abnormal. We wanted to make something that would operate on several levels. In the film we are trying to do it through an emotional response, in the installation it's a sensual and phenomenological response and in the book and CD-ROM we are trying to engage an enquiring or intellectual response.

It's about encouraging people to question those prejudices themselves, which is a much harder thing to do than being didactic and saying, "You shouldn't call someone like Eden disabled – you should think of her as being differently-abled". And its true, she is differently-abled. She does have palpable physical complications in her life but she is not deficient as a person. Eden is as full a person as you and I and anyone is. It's just that part of her body doesn't function very well, and that happens to be the bit between her intellectually average brain and the rest of her body. Many people would look at her and think that she's some kind of abnormality, not even a full person. But this not true, indeed she is physically handicapped but by no means mentally disabled. And that is the key, how can we make something which stops people from jumping to conclusions and making value judgements about a person based on how they look as opposed to what's really going on? We are not trying to answer everything in a single piece of work – it's many layered, it's complicated, with huge issues – so we are trying to deal with them in different ways with different outcomes.

Our perceptions seem to be based on a myriad of binary opposites. Our society thinks in terms of normal versus abnormal, able versus disabled, efficient versus deficient and groups people in those different camps. Yet this project very much fits into the grey area in-between.

That is something which is also important for me, existing within that grey area is one of the key things that I have always attempted to do. It goes back to a film installation I made ten years ago called *Basement Room Reflections*. I created a series of film installations, which involved projecting negative film onto a silvered glass window. It was concerned with this space between the chthonic and the terrestrial world, between the underworld and the everyday. The installation functioned as a series of hinges between one space and another, between physical space and conceptual space. I wrote a text to accompany it about an experience I had in North Africa where I was travelling in the desert and I reached a point where the desert met the ocean. For me this was the most incredible conceptual space. There was no clear distinction between the Atlantic Ocean and the Sahara Desert, the two just met. There was rock and water with no in between, just this space between them that keeps them separate, like an incredibly thin membrane that allows them to keep enough of their natures. You can't really describe it, and that for me was why it was so profound, because the space between them wasn't visible. That exploration of the spaces between, where you can't quite define where one becomes the other, is absolutely important in my work. It becomes a default position, particularly in this project, because it is about so many things, which are truths in themselves, yet held separate by their natures, so that one truth isn't muddied in another.

What is interesting is that we don't have a complete picture of Eden's cognitive abilities since we don't have the necessary means to measure them, simply because they are different to ours. Such visualising abilities are expressed in the way she dreams, paints and draws. Could this be a whole new gamut of expertise that she has, that we can't perceive?

What I think would be really wonderful would be to see how a project like *Mapping Perception* could stimulate

the kind of intervention that would enable somebody like Eden to function to their best ability in society. Where they can offer not what we think her best abilities are, but what she thinks her best abilities are. Which might be as a storyteller, as an interpreter. I can see how we might learn to appreciate a person like Eden with her amazing ability to float between memory and experience because of her partial separation from physical experience. There is this physical gap for her, from her mental abilities and her brain sending commands to her body and her body being able to carry out those functions. What kind of skill might that give her as a kind of translator between different spaces? The challenge is there for us to make it easier for people like Eden to discover how they can interact with society in a way where *they* are best served by culture and society.

It requires a whole re-evaluation of what we consider to be intelligence and what we consider to be perfection.

If *Mapping Perception* really hits the mark, it will be to challenge people to say, "These people aren't disabled, they have the possibility to be truly understood and appreciated as differently-abled. We just have to make allowances for the fact that they can't walk, or they require us to help them do things that we find easy. But they can help us do things that we can't do, or don't have access to". Not everyone has that vivid ability to interpret things in the way that Eden interprets her memory as a kind of dream state, which I think is supremely powerful. If you look in every culture, storytellers are absolutely key in our ability to make sense of the world. And isn't it doubly ironic that someone like Eden is perceived by society as not being able to make sense of the world when in fact she is able to make sense of it in a wholly unique and culturally valuable way.

There is scene in the film in which Eden is playing in the bath with a model of a brain and her Barbie shoes nearby. It seems to ask, should you look at Eden as someone with something wrong with her brain or should you look at her as any other 14 year-old girl? It is a very simplistic but powerful visual notion.

Barbie crops up again and again in the film because she represents perfection and the commercial ideal of womanhood. It's funny that a child who isn't 'perfect' is just as susceptible to those ideals as any other little girl at that age. If you think that Eden is fourteen, and Barbie is still popular within that age group, then she is behaving like a normal young teenage girl. It is also interesting to think about how Eden sees Barbie, what her perception is. Does she see Barbie as representing something she aspires to be like, or does she see Barbie as just fun, as a toy? For many girls growing up, Barbie represents a restrictive straight jacket that, combined with peer pressure, forces them to conform to an artificial ideal of how they should look and behave.

So in that way is she more free than any of us were growing up?

Or is she not? Is she just as trapped as the rest of us? An interesting question is then to ask whether normality is conferred as much by our learned behavioural weaknesses as by anything physical inherited from birth.

The film starts with and repeats an image of Eden looking out at us through binoculars. I would like to see the world from her perspective, because we are looking at the binoculars from the other way round.

It is meant to stand for her looking out at the world and also a reflexive moment. There is a lot of footage of her looking at images of herself when she was younger in the film. Even though the film was made by Andrew and Mark, this becomes a space for Eden to have a kind of authorial voice. When Andrew was going through all of his footage of her, she was actually with him quite a lot. She loves watching film of herself. I think she finds it absolutely fascinating. It's the mind-body split – "Is that me?" I think for Eden it is really interesting to look at herself outside of herself, because she physically has a mind-body split. I am also fascinated by the degrees of complexity in the film. "How does Eden perceive film of herself knowing her own condition?"

The Castle of the Five Senses is beautifully explored in the film. What do you think of it as an analogy of where we live and where Eden lives in the world?

The world is so rich, if we had different senses we would perceive it differently. But normality to us is the castle of the five senses and it is a castle because we are locked within it, trapped within it.

It was Mark who came up with the analogy, which is both literary and poetic and yet refers back to what he would call hard science and hard scientific fact. It was the result of many discussions, conversations and arguments we had over the years. At this point Mark clicked with ideas that Andrew and I were talking about. As soon as he could see it in terms of the scientific rationale it made sense to him. It is, I think, a brilliant analogy for the dilemma we face in understanding perception.

In the film, it's dealt with in a humourous way where, after Eden has climbed through a huge castle she says that she didn't like the castle because it hurt her feet. It's reduced to a moment of comedy, humour and parody. Eden is not locked within the usual Castle of the Five Senses, she is in another space altogether – her own – but trying to make her fit within it, hurts her, hurts her feet. I like that. It is a really subtle but beautiful moment in the film where there is this recognition that we are as trapped as we think Eden is. But actually she is somewhere else. She is in this space between that you can't quite define.

So is Eden one of those people who can walk that space between the paranormal and the normal?

I suspect that is where she lives, in the space between. I think the problem with our Western society is always to see people like Eden as deficient, rather than to see them as having possibility. She is clearly imbued with

possibility and it is up to us to create the interfaces to allow people like her to communicate the benefits of that possibility to us. If we are normal and they are abnormal, then it is up to us to make to make it easy for them. Not in a patronising way because we can't understand them, but because they are the exception. And that for me is what this project is about. That's why at the beginning of the process we talked about it being a social project, that we wanted to influence society. We didn't just want to make a gorgeous piece of art that could be put in a gallery. People quite often see something that is socially engaged in an art gallery but they won't necessarily take it on board personally as something they need to think about it terms of their relationship with society. We want *Mapping Perception* to initiate a change in the relationships that ordinary people have with disability and abnormality.

There is a strange sci-fi fantasy that human beings could become perfect, free from disease or disability, which I think is very problematic. It must be a very profound thing for people with disabilities now to hear that scientists could one day design babies that don't have disabilities. Frankly I suspect that real applications of such technology are several generations away. We know how to disassemble genetic structures, but we are still very poor at repairing genes in the human body itself.

Difference is neither good, nor true, nor false, nor bad. We are creatures in a state of constant evolution. Evolution might creep over thousands of years but that shouldn't mean that we should start tinkering with it now to make ourselves perfect. Because we will probably mess it up in the long term. We just don't know enough. For many of people it is that very subjective desire for everyone to be perfect and normal, which is itself scary and based on fear. Why should we be afraid of having hardship? Is it because we are afraid of the unknown, afraid of things that are unquantifiable? The issues here are social and cultural, not merely technical. Just because we have the ability to do something is not an ethical or moral reason to do it.

This is in addition to whatever other riches our society would lose by terminating such lives if this mindset was dominant.

Christy Brown was a famous writer who suffered from Cerebral Palsy (the author of *Down All the Days*), made famous when he was portrayed in the movie *My Left Foot*. He was significantly physically disabled yet possessed a brilliant mind. Several works of astonishing cultural importance were produced as a result of his life. And this film definitely changed the way people saw 'spastics'. It made them think differently. What would we do without that, or Christopher Nolan's *Under the Eye of the Clock*? I see *Mapping Perception* as an attempt to articulate the reasons why we need to change our society. Not just in terms of how we look at people but also thinking fundamentally about what causes us to look at people in a disparaging way.

We tend to hide from difference and hide different people away. In our recent history and even now to an extent we still do not welcome a fully integrated society.

When you go back in history, people with disabilities often did not survive as long as they do today. In the middle ages, they were called God's Children and it was the duty of all communities to look after them. It is only with the advent of capitalism in the West that they started to be hidden away. There are numerous books about this, for instance, Michel Foucault addresses this in *The Birth of the Clinic* and *Madness and Civilisation*. In terms of architectural history, if you look at 19th century Municipal architecture and the hospitals, prisons and old peoples homes built between 1960-1990, they are built on the same principles. They are all prisons.

How much do you think our society has moved on from so many of the perceptions put forth in the archival footage in the film?

Not much. Some of the archive sound samples and the video clips in the film are from the 40s, 50s and 60s and obviously attitudes have changed since then. We have become a more understanding society, which is to be thankful for. But I also feel that we are a long, long way from where I think the aims of the project would like us to be, which is a much more open and tolerant society, tolerant of difference. We may live in one of the most tolerant societies in the world, but it is still riven with prejudices and injustices. I see this project as attempting in its own little way to make a contribution to promoting more understanding.

It is a huge undertaking to challenge people's perceptions of disability. Mapping Perception, provides a personal perspective and an intimate window into the individual, that is Eden. This is in opposition to the category of 'otherness', with which it is so easy to see people with disabilities as a homogeneous mass. Was this idea pivotal to the concept of individual disorientation being developed for the installation?

We do see such people as a group but they are not. Individual conditions affect people in a similar way, but the individual is affected profoundly in different ways. For a lot people with these kinds of illnesses like Joubert Syndrome, Cerebral Palsy, Parkinsons or Alzheimers, there are treatments and therapies, but they have to be individually tailored because they strike people in different ways. We are so used to bunching people together, pigeon-holing them as the 'other', yet they are all uniquely different. Thus we never really get to grips with what that difference might be, except that it is different, 'other' to our own experiences. This kind of approach is really hard to change and frustrating for all of us because it is a cultural norm we all grow up with. I aspire not to think like that myself, but I know it affects me as much as anyone else. That in unguarded moments I find myself in the grip of unreasonable prejudice.

It was very much in response to these issues that the installation concept was developed – it's about taking people outside the safe boundaries they are normally engaged within and placing them in a space where their spaces are disrupted abnormally. We are trying to suggest what it is like to not have access to your senses in a way you normally use them. It's about giving people a taste of a different world.

But is it not just awareness? We naturally learn a socially conditioned behaviour but if we are switched on to suddenly think about it, to become aware of it, that can be huge step in making a difference.

The aim of the project was to create a series of moments that would make people aware of themselves in relation to difference. And that is what the project really aims to do – to *make* people aware by creating a space for feeling and reflection, not to tell them that they *should* be aware. It doesn't aim to place a value judgement on how people think, but to inspire empathy. Feeling can short circuit prejudice.

And it's not empathising for, but empathising *with*. I hope the project inspires its audiences to feel some sort of equality of experience with people such as Eden. That just as they muddle on with their lives so she muddles on with hers, and that is the human condition, neither better nor worse, just different. Each experience has its own value and it is essential that we learn to appreciate the value of other people's experience rather than being afraid of difference and living in fear and ignorance of the richness that it should bring.

Prolix Persiflage – Janna Levin

I've started talking to myself. Voluble speeches, thick bubbled words, rages, the grocery list. There's nothing too insignificant nor too personal to rant out-loud. I don't remember when it first became a struggle to seal the window between my own perception and the outside world. But I'm sure there was a time, not so long ago, when I didn't habitually converse with myself with quite such intensity, with such commitment to the conversation. I actually become offended if interrupted. Is this normal? The outside world used to influence my inner dialogue but now that inner dialogue has leaked all gooey and transparent onto the world out there.

I can't stop the torrent of words. Just language, the urge to speak. I wake up first thing in the morning and even as I pry myself out of my melatonin haze, I start mumbling. Not like sleep-talking. More like a tourets interjection – a comment or two between the reality of coffee and waking life and the day's plans. In some awkward way my early morning behaviour reminds me of Eden, her torrent of sounds, the spill of language, the child's shear urge to speak. But surely I'm normal. As far as I am aware, I do have a complete serving of cerebellum. I believe my perception of the world to be somewhat accurate. But this is the lame self-evaluation that Mark and Andrew abandoned. Clearly Eden's physical departure from normalcy, however brazenly you define such a thing, is simply identifiable: she is missing a piece of her cerebellum. But here we watch her dissected, analysed, we watch her playing and we try to figure out who this little girl is and how she perceives the world. Regardless of how much information is accumulated and ordered we are conspicuously weak on meaningful conclusions. Along the way, inevitably, our own confidences about perception and normalcy get screwed up.

But I don't want to worry about the accuracy of my perception of the world. This is life. If we dissect our perception too forensically life's basic pleasures curdle into the mundane and the tedious. 'Murdering to dissect' is, I think, the catch phrase. It's just consciousness. I wake up, yabber to myself and without intention carry on with the interpretation of the world that I left behind when I dropped off to sleep the night before. Maybe there's some continuity, a gently ruffled perception of the world. And so it goes day after day. Interpreting the world, figuring my place in it, the meaning of it all, the unbearable purposelessness. Always trying to understand, to think, to explain, to know. For all of its fuzziness and all of my strange behaviour – I am after all talking to myself, even now my lips are actually moving as I type – I accept my picture of the world and it seems to get me through most situations. Like Eden, I don't particularly care if I'm normal. Look how she plays. Look how she splashes in the bath. Look how she's a child.

The night of the first preview screening of *Mapping Perception* I was thinking things like this. I was braced for what Mark and Andrew were plotting. Don't even think you're going to manipulate my emotions I warn

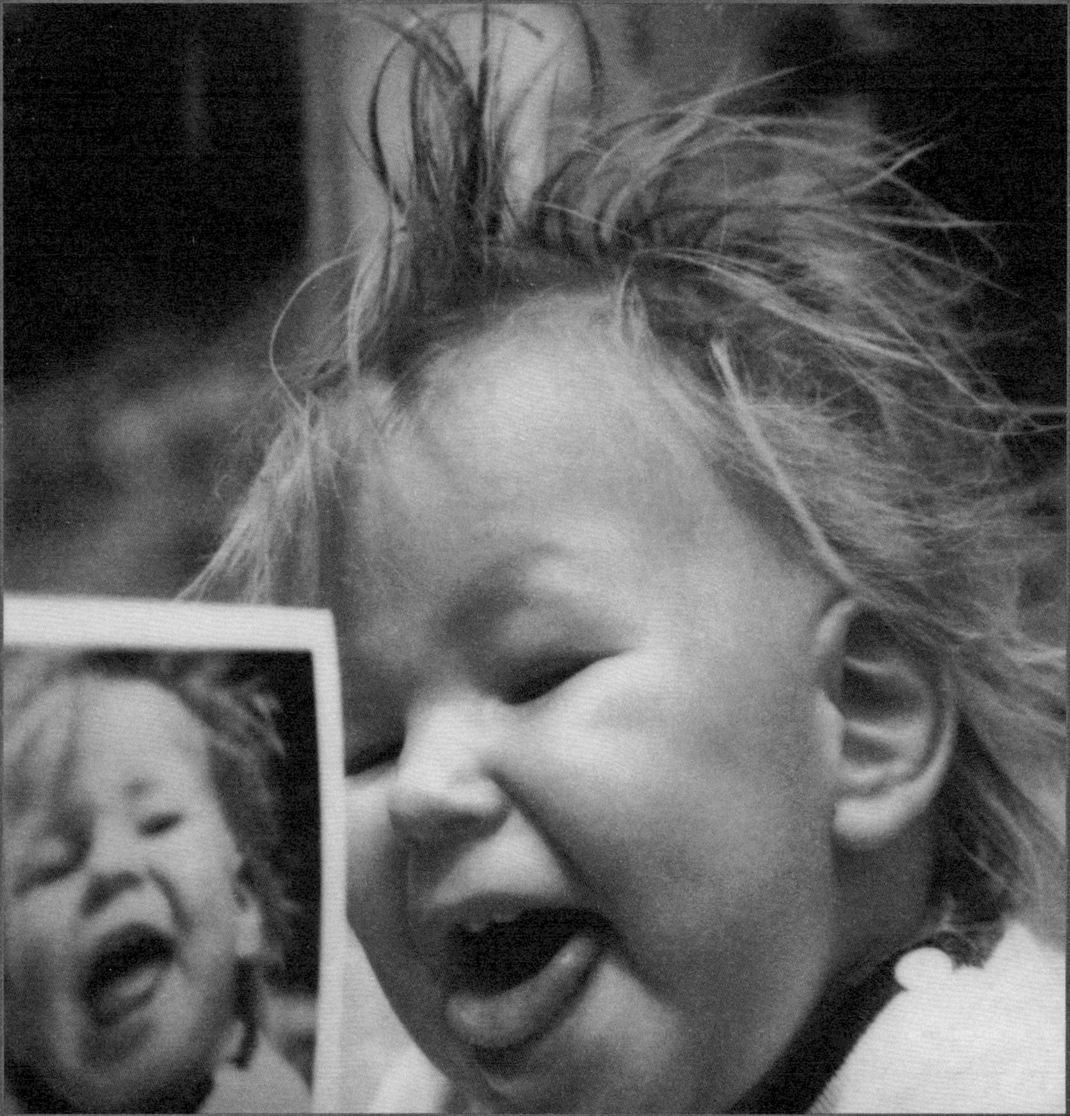

Eden, 1988

Eden & Leila

Eden & Andrew

them by the look on my face, mentally pointing a finger at them. Grumbling to myself I squish into my chair and await the screening. Of course this is all mock surliness. I trust them both and am not disappointed. The film doesn't indulge in moral outrage or clichèd swipes at normalcy and it's defendants. Neither Andrew nor Mark have the luxury of such superficial positions. They just erode our complacency with a jarring ambiguity. Jagging film, blurry images, shifty eyes, strange sounds, the ever protruding tongue.

Mark and Andrew were so anxious to see the world through Eden's eyes that Mark wanted to inject a brain paralysing drug into his own neck. The effects are temporary he assures me eagerly. (Too eagerly I think. This makes me worry for him.) Andrew takes the suggestion seriously but then thinks better of it, remembers his familial role, and regains his footing. So, luckily, nobody injects anybody in the neck with a brain atrophying, or rather, paralysing drug. But they work hard to see the world through Eden's eyes when we know that they can't even see the world through each other's eyes. But it's the futility of the exercise that's the lesson. And by then they have me wondering about perception.

But surely I can get through the world without such fruitless doomed self-inspection. So what if nobody's normal, if nobody knows the world or each other. I feel placated as they pat me on the back reassuringly. Sure, sure, sure. But I can only stave off the images for so long.

Like Mark, I'm drawn to science and the answers science provides. There's a ruthless impatience scientists have for extraneous bits and bobs. I know how to pare perception down to its minimal form: to receive information about the external world without deforming it too overtly in the process. Nature doesn't need embellishing. She provides a genuinely mesmerizing story. Atoms were synthesized in the big bang and then stars formed and billions of years on in history there's a fresh planet made of stars' debris with Carbon and Oxygen and Amino Acids and cells and life and genes and human beings and mutations and evolution. It's a stupefying and gorgeous epic. Each of us is an enormously complex execution of a list of chromosome pairs and a gene alphabet. And the reductionist in me realizes that this could be the whole story. This is me. My condition, my normalcy, is the unique product of my mother's genes and my father's genes. And their genetic score was written and rewritten through generations back to the origins of time itself. And I wake up gauging if this is the sum total of who I am? I think that might have been what I said this morning: "Is this who I am?" I burst this non sequitor off toward the windows shaking my head in contradiction in between an ordinary conversation about whether or not I wanted coffee.

My day begins prodded by Eden to play out one of her scenes. In the film, Eden explains to us that she is the unique product of her mother's genes and her father's genes. Her beautiful, sultry mother Leila and her virile, brickhouse of a father Andrew. By rights, what an impressive physical specimen they should have produced. The throw of the dice, the peculiar linking of one gene to the next, and Eden is born in all of her complicated, wondrous Edenness. Even as she explains to us about Joubert Syndrome, she seems easily aware that she is not the sum total of her medical condition. Or maybe easily unaware of the burden of these interpretations. And while her explanation knocks the breath out of me, as though she is calmly explaining a train wreck that brought her into the world, I don't ever feel sorry for her.

This is Andrew's doing. Andrew gives us no easy opportunity to feel pity, tragedy or even a clean sadness. There's nothing sentimental about this film. Nothing desperate or despairing and oddly, really oddly, nothing tragic. The film weaves in snippets from Andrew's diary

kept of Eden's birth, her early medical notes and her diagnosis, a heart-sinking condemnation. Neurological problems. Joubert Syndrome of cerebellar vermis hypoplasia. But the film mocks this too. It is obvious that for all of the medical information, this is not Eden. Eden is just a complicated little girl with strange layers of speech, self-awareness, and a happy child's giggle when she catches her own image in the mirror. And still they come to hear more. More medical reports, more gene studies, more prognoses.

The film is not dismissive of science either, not at all. Science isn't bad. Science is clankingly hollow sometimes, and inadequate always, but not quite morally bad. Andrew and Leila needed, desired, longed for, an accurate diagnosis of their daughter. And they obsessed over the medical reports. Their absurd Latin conglomerates that came out with an emotion that wasn't intended. They need these reports and they needed to understand them but clearly it was never enough. And they embrace and integrate science's conclusions just as Andrew embraces Mark as neurophysiologist to try to compile a woefully inadequate picture of Eden but it doesn't matter because the film is not about Eden.

Mark and Andrew come back from a trip to the Joubert Foundation conference in New Orleans and Mark produces for me a photograph of Andrew dancing with his daughter. The look on Andrew's face in this simple moment is an archetypal depiction of the loving father. This great big bear of a man, with his steady eyes and his robust laugh and his toughness, his real live toughness, bending over to dance with his fourteen year old daughter, she's all concentration and he is covered with a private and frankly happy grin. He's just the loving father. Mark hands it to me and declares, "That says it all".

Eden & Andrew, New Orleans, July 2022

Revelations – Mark Lythgoe

Mapping Perception is a distillation or approximation of four years of conversation and collaboration with Andrew (1) and Eden Kötting, Giles Lane et al. Before I met Andrew, I had been involved with several science and art (sci-art) collaborations and had become a little tired of seeing the same old sci-art work that inevitably meant that the artist came into the scientist's work space, took some pretty pictures off the computer and stuck them in a art gallery. These exhibitions were for me just that, pretty pictures on the wall, not cutting edge contemporary art – whatever that maybe. On the flip side of this, I was also a little frustrated with today's scientific documentaries and their gratuitous use of graphics, which bore no resemblance to the facts presented and I would regularly find that I could never remember a single image from a programme or how they had contributed to it. Although I didn't know what I wanted out of a sci-art collaboration, I was quite clear that any further projects would have to be on a different footing, a mutually inclusive project in which language, communication and understanding was at the heart. The process of tool gathering for the challenge ahead

carried on for about a year and a half. It was obvious that the language used within science was poles apart from that offered in the art world. This was our first point of focus – the exchange of language – which was not an easy or comfortable process, as language is underpinned by our cultural and social context, as well as our own personal misgivings about our world. Andrew took me to exhibitions and I escorted him to brain lectures. During a lecture on the developmental biology of the cerebellum, Andrew slipped me a note that made me smile. It read 'Could you translate some of this confabulate over lunch please. Because it means nothing to me'. In time Andrew became an integral member of our department, comfortably chatting away to the various scientists about topics such as football (especially with my boss who is big Manchester United supporter), art, disability, money, jobs and even quantum mechanics or neuronal migration.

In turn, Andrew introduced me to his filmic buddies Dan Weldon, Ben Woolford and Sean Lock at the production house Tall Stories. My early lessons involved filming, editing, online, offline, film formats, DV cam, Beta SP, Super 8, Final Cut Pro, etc. This essential training equipped me for the process of collecting, collating and cataloguing hundreds of samples and the laborious process of connecting an image or clip with one of the hundreds of voices. The narrative for *Mapping Perception* was created not via a series of happenstance events, but was formed like a jigsaw– piece by piece, trial and error – until the story we had in our collective unconscious was realised. Those were the moments of revelation for me. That blinding flash (as used in the installation) when everything pours out from the melting pot to leave that pure element behind. I cannot explain how or why you suddenly get those moments of clarity, when that fuzzy fog inside your head finally lifts. It is those moments when you know you have not travelled the normal route of A to B to C, but rather, have been able to jump straight to Z, without using the stepping-stones in between. What a moment of joy when you reach that place, it can only be compared to the view from Cadirs Idris on a sunny winter's day. This is what I get up for in the morning. This is why I suffer the anguish and frustration of research. This is where the real commonality lies in both science and art.

Alongside this extraordinary exchange and at the heart of this work was Eden, Andrew's daughter, who suffers from the rare condition, Joubert Syndrome. One of the aims of our research was to take a look at the world through Eden's eyes. By combining both science and art in a mutually inclusive fashion, we hoped to create a new metaphor that might bring us closer to the core substance of what we perceive in ourselves and others. From the outset of the collaboration we realised that neither art nor science in their own rights had the language or understanding to answer certain questions, such as 'What would the world look like through Eden's eyes?' or 'What is love?'. It was out of the understanding that some tools are just not appropriate for the job in hand, that it was necessary to provide a new window through which to investigate the thin membrane between the able and the disabled. *Mapping Perception*

started out as an experiment – an experimental documentary – born out of the belief that the combination of two personalities from distinct disciplines may find a way to blur the boundaries between normality and abnormality.

Believe only half of what you see, and nothing
of what you hear.
Dinah Craik (1858).

Visual Perception

The opening sequence of the film and elements within the installation focus on the visual system and asks, 'Is what you see what you get?'. Through experience we learn to perceive or understand what we're looking at and we get used to how things are supposed to be. Sometimes our brains get the clues all wrong and other times, our brains fill in the missing pieces. In 1870, while reading a book on sound, L. Hermann saw grey spots in the intersections of spaces among the figures that were arranged in a matrix (2). It is now known that they're caused by the way your eyes respond to light and dark areas. When an area is surround by light, your eye compensates by 'turning down' the brightness (3),

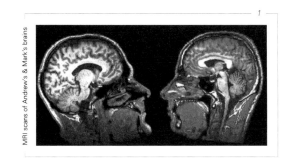

MRI scans of Andrew's & Mark's brains

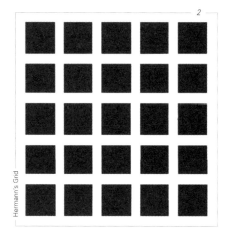

Hermann's Grid

making you see darkened areas. In this grid, the areas surrounded by the most white are at the intersections of the white lines. Since this phenomenon, known as lateral inhibition, works best in your peripheral vision, the spots disappear when you look right at them. If dark areas are brightened and light areas turned down, why then does a checkerboard look as though it has black and white squares? Part of the answer is a filling-in or abstraction (see later), which is quite similar to that which occurs in the blind spot, where the eye fills in information that it cannot see (4). Understanding the way in which an object should look, the brain is able to compensate for the missing information by making-up the intensity between the two squares and completing the checkerboard.

Lateral inhibition networks largely operate as part of the unconscious brain, without communicating what they are doing to the conscious part. Visual signals that we receive are modified by the nervous system (abstractions) to provide images of the world around us.

These abstractions are based on our knowledge of stable, constant external forms with well defined edges; in fact this percept is so strong that the nervous system will try to create boundaries (5). These percepts may even define what are seen as the human experience of ideal forms. Such ideal forms are, as William Blake has described, not from observations of nature but from inner visions, that is, the abstractions in our brain, which may be the very essence of either art or science – the ability to abstract.

Another illusion, which is one of my favourites, is the rotating mask, which has a hollow (negative) version that immediately switches back into a positive or normal view of the face (6). The reason you find it difficult to visualise the hollow version, is that a normal face is such a strong percept that it overcomes the history of rotation – the only cue that the face is negative. If such quick and dirty tricks are able to fool our senses, one must ask what does the world really look like and how different is my view to that of others

To find your blind spot, close your LEFT eye and stare straight at the CROSS whilst moving the book towards and away from you. The circle should disappear as it falls into the blind spot. Both eyes possess an area where the retina is missing (the blind spot) which the brain compensates for to complete an normal uninterrupted field of view

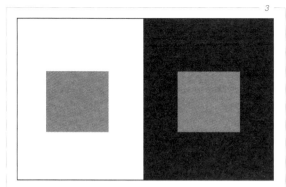

grey squares appear to have different
intensities yet are the same, an effect of
lateral inhibition.

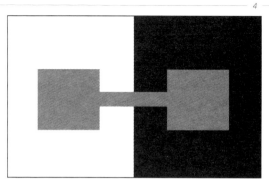

an illusion of a boundary formed in the
centre grey rectangle, an effect of
abstraction in the brain.

Normal Convex Hollow Normal Hollow Concave

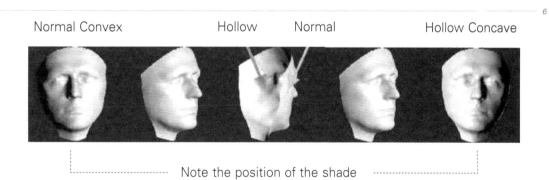

Note the position of the shade

A sequence of individual stills taken from an animation of a rotating mask by
Isabelle & Heinrick Bulthoff. As the mask rotates it always appears convex, just
like a normal face, even thought it is concave for half its rotation. The percept of
a convex human face is so strong, as not to allow the observer to visualise the
concave situation.

The Voice of Science

Thirteen years after Eden left hospital, Andrew, Leila and I went down to Guy's Hospital to read through her early investigations and findings. The notes describes in a somewhat, cold and clinical fashion the events that followed after an emergency caesarean section, 'Failure to progress, foetal distress, emergency caesarean section... we will see her again in one year's time.' At the age of one, another clinical report issued the statement 'intellectual function will be better than is at present obvious' – a note of hope from the hospital. It is these reports that now provided the backdrop to the initial scenes in the film of Eden as a baby and emphasises the difficulties to provide the correct diagnosis in these very rare conditions.

The voice of science is visually embodied in the recreation of *The Anatomy Lesson of Dr Nicholas Tulp* by Rembrandt (circa 1632) (7). The image pertains to an era of great anatomical discovery together with meticulous documentation through drawings or wax models. It was a time when the community would be entertained with the thrills of the public dissections. A time exemplified by Leonardo Da Vinci when science and art were as one. A rotating MRI brain imaging together with blood vessels is used in the background of the scene as a reminder that in 350 B.C. Aristotle considered that the heart was the seat of the mental processes and the brain served as a cooling agent for the heart.

7

production still

Eden's View of the World

Seeing the world through Eden's eyes was never going to be an easy task. Andrew had filmed Eden since the day she was born and by combining this with all the clinical, and scientific research that described Eden and Joubert Syndrome, we hope to create a picture of Eden's world. Eden was diagnosed by Brian Neville, now based at the Great Ormond Street Hospital (GOSH) and currently she attends both the neurology and behavioural clinics at GOSH. Andrew and I have spoken with many of the scientists that have seen Eden, yet even from their comprehensive accounts it was not always that easy to gauge what it was like in Eden's inner world. Some investigations gave us an indication of how well she could see: 'shoe at three metres; spoon, banana at two metres; cup and watch at one metre'. Other descriptions, despite their attention to detail, were far more elusive: visual impairment with bilateral ptosis, gazed-evoked nystagmus, impaired up-gaze, impaired visual acuity, optic atrophy and a pigmentary retinopathy; cerebellar ataxia; hypotonia and ligamentous laxity. There was no doubt that we had got closer to Eden, but we began to feel a certain frustration as we we're not able to 'get inside' Eden. Speaking with colleagues at GOSH and the Institute of Neurology, I learnt of two tests that may allow us the bridge to the gap into Eden's castle. My idea was that if you could 'knockout' the part of the brain that Eden is missing, you may be able to simulate a particular aspect of Joubert Syndrome. The first test I suggested that Andrew should try was the Wada test (named after the neurologist, J. A. Wada). During the test, one side of the brain is put to sleep (anaesthetised) by injecting an anaesthetic into the major artery in the neck. For example, when the drug is injected into the left carotid artery, the left side of the brain is anaesthetised for several minutes. Because the left side of the brain controls movement on the right side of the body, the right side of the body will not be able to move for this period of time. Also, if the anaesthetised side is the side that controls speech, the patient will not be able to speak until the effect of the drug clears. At GOSH the WADA test is used to determine which side of the brain language is dominant. This is performed in children with intractable epilepsy, that may go on to have a hemispherectomy (surgical removal of half the cerebrum).

The second choice I gave Andrew was to partake in a little transcranial magnetic stimulation (TMS), which uses magnetic fields produced by passing electric currents through a hand-held coil. The coil is driven by a machine that switches the large current necessary in a very precise and controlled way, at rates up to 50 cycles per second. The coil is held on the scalp – no actual contact is necessary – and the magnetic field passes through the skull and into the brain. Small induced currents can then make brain areas below the coil more or less active. In practice, TMS is able to influence many brain functions, including movement, visual perception, memory, reaction time, speech and mood. The effects produced are genuine but temporary, lasting only a short time after actual stimulation has stopped.

Now Andrew is not adverse to a little pain, if you look closely at the inside of his forearms you will see the fine detail of brandings performed with an hot iron. One of the first of Andrew's adornments I noticed were the tattoos on his ankles and calves. At first glance they look like inky line drawings describing the satellite system around Alpha-ketone-rhubarb. On closer inspection I found that Andrew had permanently transcribed Eden's first line drawings into his calves. Yet despite the fact that Andrew would gladly go twelve rounds just for the pleasure of the pain, I still couldn't quite get him to have that little part of his brain 'scientifically knocked out'.

The Castle of the Five Senses

I described to Andrew and Giles that the way we perceive with the world was through our fives senses: taste, touch, hearing, seeing and smelling. (Although there are some who talk about the sense of time and a sense of falling, and also the sixth sense – the ability to identify chemicals called pheromones that are secreted by many animals.) I went on to suggest that being human is like being locked in the Castle of our Five Senses (8). Each of the fives senses are represented by the narrow windows from which archers could defend against an oncoming attack. If for example we take the visual system, one castle window would represent visible light from which we could view the world around. However, the brickwork around the window represents the rest of the electromagnetic spectrum (e.g. ultra violet, infrared, x-ray, radiowaves) which we as human we are not privy. So being human means that we only have a very narrow view into the world and as we have seen earlier (in Visual Perception above), the senses that we rely on so heavily to inform us of our world, such as the visual system, are easily deceived. We carried on this discussion while we were on holiday in France and it was then we filmed Eden on her adventure to the top of Queribus Castle (9).

We were not designed to see outside our window of visible light, but certain species of birds can see ultraviolet light, which is just beyond what people can see at the end of the rainbow spectrum where you see blue and violet, and is used to help in foraging and mate choice. Insects such as bees and ants make the proverbial beeline back to their nests using polarized light sensors to detect the north-south attitude of polarisation as it scatters through the atmosphere. (Polarised light – think of light as arrows with feathers at one end for flight stability. Even when the arrows are travelling in the same direction, their tail feathers are rotating. When the tail feathers line up in the same direction, the light is said to be polarized.) Bees also communicate with each other via dancing. The dance tells the precise information about direction and distance to the food source. Because the position of the sun changes during the day, the dance angle must also change; and this actually occurs. If the sun is concealed behind clouds or terrain, the bee analyses the pattern of polarised light from the sky. A particular intensity of polarised light is generated toward the earth's surface from every point in the sky, and so the sun's position is determined by the bee's sensitivity to polarisation differences. In the second half of the film, it is Eden, whilst sitting on her swing, who raises the final uncertainty when she asks, "And what would my feet look like in polarised light?"

In 2001, Richard Gregory wrote an editorial (Perception, 2001; 30: 903) based on his book (*Mirrors in Mind*, 1996) where he poses the question, "How does one recognise one's own face, though never seen except in a mirror?" He was referring to the fact that the only time we see ourselves is in a mirror, and as this image is a reflection that is reversed left to right, we never see our true self (see Richard Gregory below). In the project Eden uses the mirror to look at herself, and within these reflections are her memories of past experiences.

Queribus Castle, France

film stills

Today Eden climbed 482 steps to the top of Queribus castle

Soundscape

Toby McMillan created much of the soundtrack from
recordings taken during research studies in the
1 experimental and clinical magnetic resonance imaging
(MRI) scanners at the Great Ormond Street Hospital
and Institute of Child Health (10 & 11). Listening to
the curious soundtrack, you not only get a feel for the
peculiarities of an MRI scanner, but also the unusual
properties of sound via the intense resonances in the
ear. This effect may alter depending on where you are
in space when listening to the soundtrack. The frequency of the sound is such that areas of cancellation
or increases in volume may be heard, similar to the
effect when dropping two pebble into a pond, some
of the ripples will cancel, others will be additive,
leading to columns of sound distributed within the
gallery space.

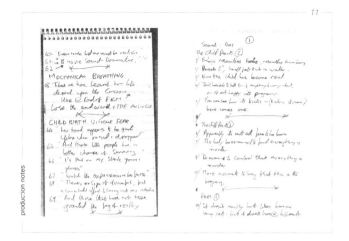

10

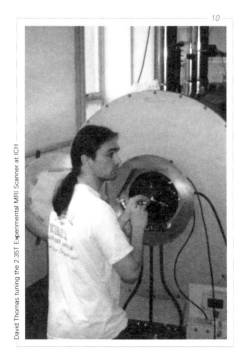

David Thomas tuning the 2.35T Experimental MRI Scanner at ICH

11

MECHANICAL BREATHING
CHILD BIRTH WITHOUT FEAR

production notes

Conclusion

In true science fashion you get a conclusion, not that there really is any conclusion. The *Mapping Perception* project is the crystallisation of four years' work. The fractionation of the love affair that initially produced the film, and which was then further refined and purified to produce the installation. These pieces of work are put forward as the best approximations or agents that offer a window of opportunity to cast light on the penumbra of our perception.

Mapping Perception was never meant to rest comfortably on anyone's shoulders; it is meant to question what is at the heart of others and ourselves. Some may find the work uncomfortable or painful, this was not contrived but rather a result of the natural time course of our collaboration. Those difficult moments have always served to raise questions within and about our own situation, ideals or values and it is out of those difficult moments that we find laughter is the antidote to the emotions of life with which we are uneasy or we do not understand.

A Little Disgurgative Confabulate – Andrew Kotting

By way of an introduction I offer you a back story.
(These notes culled from eversowayback before we had the knowing.)

Leila, 1987

fig: 1987
Our smell and then her conception. 13.6.87
A veritable Cupid's gymnasium.
A travelling year. A magical year.
Leila is pregnant and we prepare for Africa:
Kenya and then Madagascar, land of man eating trees.
Hubbub in the Baobabs
We pack a book and I read.

The trouble with being born.

EM Cioran: *Never comfortable in the immediate,*
I am lured only by what precedes me, what distances me from here,
the numberless moments when I was not: the non-born.

Madagascar, 1987

Andrew Kötting, 1987

I make a series of drawings around the themes of pregnancy and normality. I am put in mind of my oldest brother Peter, an achondroplastic, a dwarf; big torso with short arms and legs. Strong like a *pig*.

Leila gives birth to **Eden** Rintoul McMillan **Kötting**.
An emergency caesarean section.

Andrew Kötting, 1987

Failure to progress. Foetal distress. Resuscitation, mucus extraction and oxygen by mask.
High pitched weak cry. Slight grasp. No further comments on baby's condition.

And it doesn't exactly look like a human being yet but it has a heart that beats.

Stable relationship for 6 years, father student, 3 bedroom council flat.
Mother unemployed. Caucasian 26 year old. Mum and dad visited and aware of condition.

You do realise that this little girl might be unaware that she has this disease?

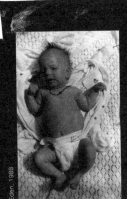

Eden, 1988

Seems hungry but will not suck. Seen by neurologist. No problems.
Eden to be discharged, home by pm. Health visitor informed.
Some investigations have been arranged for baby.
Visual problems. Jerky eye movements, almost a nystagmus.
Ultra sound head: The brain looks normal with normal SYE?
Possibly slightly Compressed. No hydrocephalus. No haemorrhage.
CT scan : progress poor doesn't seem to see.

Hey steady on, you're not going to help a patient if you're in a panic. Now try again.

Occasional smile. Parents were in Africa for 2 months during pregnancy.
Dad's brother achondroplasia. Global problems otherwise in good health. Generally happy.
Can sometimes sit. Squashed looking with no head control. Insults across the neurological board.

Now the child has become more **real.**

She is the first child born to healthy and unrelated parents and therefore there
is a major genetic issue about this diagnosis. I saw both parents and explained the
uncertainties of the diagnosis. I will give them some further information since they
are intelligent people who would otherwise be trying to get further information about
this from their own reading

A simple little examination and it doesn't hurt, you lie quietly relaxed whilst the doctor has a good look at you and it's soon over.

I saw Eden in my clinic today. I am pleased to say that she is doing well.
Eden's visual acuity is very unlikely to improve with this condition and in fact
it may well deteriorate. The brain looks normal, possibly slightly compressed ventricles.
We will see her again in one year.

Neurological deficits and defects in the genetic code.
All this occurring during the course of embryonic development. In vitro.
Neurological agenesis as just not getting it together. Gone, away with the fairies.
Sounds of Esther Lamandier, Morton Feldman, Stella Chiwesha and David Darling.
Today in Senate House Library I was watching Academia with all it's internal compulsion.
Deep in the thinking to the exclusion of almost everything.
Their intellectual autism versus an emotional intelligence.
Found very little on the Syndrome or things vermis ataxia.
Where they're at.
At the moment she is biting her tongue and wearing a hat,
from Madagascar,
and letting the bile run all over her traffic light toy and then herself.
She really is a load of fun.
The bringing up baby year. The sitting in the arm chair year.
The isn't life disappointing year.
So today I decide to run the London marathon.
I'm evicted before I cross the finishing line for not having a number.

Andrew Kötting, *Herself* 1999

fig: 8.8.88

Numbers mean something on this day and Glenda Jackson swings my heart her way.
Back now again at almost eight on the eighth of the eighth, eighty eight day.
Drinking, with a chance to thinking,
fingers and the stink of the past, which always brings tears to my eyes,
and then to press ups in eight's, done for the trunk of the tree, and the memory,
of the angry cupid's gymnasium.

We're crossing the river to get to the other side, don't ask me why, the river's not wide.

The first grabbings and kickings of the baby are little more than
spastic expressions of excitement.

It echoes aqueously: sat here in the bath listening to a dear friend watching her spasticity, sighing *poorcunt*,
which makes me smile and then contemplate endlessly.
November and in Holland Eden smiled.
Medicine and the art of preserving and restoring health.
We know what is *wrong*: why sometimes she forgets to breathe.
Why her hands and feet twitch, her face convulses and her eyes rove.
Why her balance is so poor, her head nods and her tongue sticks out.
She is missing a bit of her cerebellum.
The little brain, the roast chestnut, the arbour vitae, the heart of the *matter*,
the heart of sleep, the heart of thinking, the heart of appetite and feeding,
the heart of memory and attention, the heart of motivation, movement, posture, balance and muscle tone.
Some even refer to it as the "seat of the soul"
To live with all of this and to want to find out more. To understand.
And one day I read that her life expectancy is not good and that

"few if any sufferers survived into adult hood."

I am consumed by a desire to keep a record of her life and to let her very existence inform and inspire my work.

fig: 1989
Already there is a standing frame and a naked baby strapped into position.
I am trying to feed her by spoon.
No words. Just Yogurt.
Pretending to think and the animistic presence in this the Pyrenean forest.
Hoi Polloi
Feeding my baby is like filling a very deep hole with runny Pollyfilla.
If I had money for every beakerfull of saliva she discards then I'd never go hungry.
Retard.
She is rather under the weather.
I'm depressed, except for my shoes
and a rude magazine which has just fallen onto the floor.

Eden, 1988

fig: 1990

Valgus.

```
The parents are worried about her feet. Eden can walk whilst grasping and holding on,
however she cannot walk independently because of balance problems which are probably
due to her cerebellum. Both feet look as if they are going into valgus.
```

Safe in the boots. Those Piedro boots. Sent to support her.
Postlip
Spent the night fretting about a baby with a full bowel.
Missed breakfast and then into the morning
watching burnt umber leaves,
fluttering to the ground, revealing trees,
on the edge of the woods.
The baby suckles.
She shits.
Now travelling a lot lighter in all probability.
Sounds of The Wolfgang Press and Moondog.

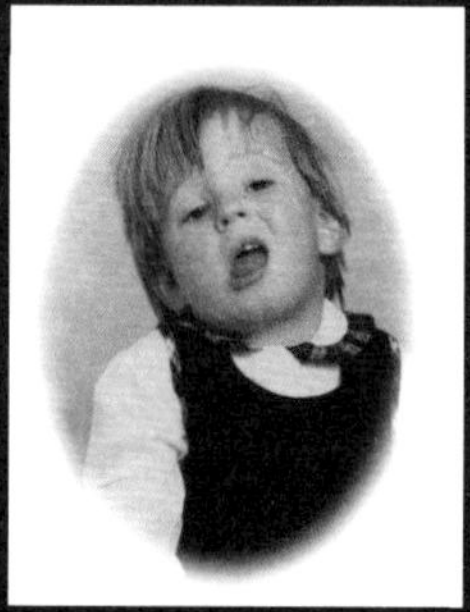

Eden school portrait, 1992

fig: 1991

Rationalising the life gives me a propensity for sanity?
On her third birthday Eden was often on the
telephone, well, her right hand was.
She also starts to stand straight.
All very late.
I wanted it to be magnificent, which it isn't,
so I'm happy with the insignificance.

Supposition

An Eden thougthover :
I'm lying here waiting,
not wanting the arriving,
happy with my fetal lining,
wishing
I was back in the balls of that maligning
swine
of a father.
(Repatriation is now impossible, given that she has her
continuum to take care of. Her name chosen over Aden
for a boy, which is where her mother, Leila, was born.
And the garden.)

fig: 1992

If only her days were like mine.
Earliest.
Which needless to say is nonsense.
No need to say.
Of days in a park kicking a ball at Grandad ;
Albert. Goalie, contented.
Peter on the wing, chasing Leesa (in the midfield
to pull out a handful of hair.
Mark at centre forward, (spent more time lying d
and Joey in defence, head up, plane spotting.
I've got the ball with just the goalie to beat.
Albert, who looks at his great grand daughter no
Relativity.
My tools and their relativity.

Absurdity and Ambiguity.
Dada and Surrealism.
Sounds of Psychic TV and John Tavener.
The car doesn't work.

Eden Kötting, 1993

fig: 1993

Lifething is about this moment: rounding it up,
herding it into the pen of memory,
too many strays. I need a dog.
Milk cows and carrots are human inventions,
like lap dogs and pebble dashed houses,
as much as steam engines and gunpowder.
Eden has started to draw.
All the time.

Sounds of Chris Watson, Goran Bregovic and Stock, Hausen, Walkman.
If only the air from her mornings were rich in determination as the young patient attempts her first uneven steps.
They're not. Today I saw Eden as a late middle aged woman, her mum and dad were gone and it
made me sad.
Smart Alek
A black trip down memory lane.

fig: 1994

La Bas
Still the painting and the decorating.
But reading and the attempting a Telling in other ways.
*How it is, my **Company.***
Past moments, old dreams back again,
or fresh like those that pass,
and things; things always memories,
I say them as I hear them in the mud.
Me the second hand thinker

Eden school portrait, 1994

Pompous audacious driveller, squirter.
Ill said. Ill heard. Ill collated. Ill assimilated. Ill regurgitated.
So I don't expect to astonish anyone, and I'm sitting down again.
Crying like a slattern,
bits
and scraps,
with nothing else to think.
If only.
Jaunt
The river Thames and
the sounds of John Wall.

Eden Kötting, 1994

fig: 1995

Him, **a twit gone drank.**

Seems ages since my hands have been inside a carcass.
I travel Britain with Gladys. She begins to understand Eden:

"If you put her on top of Buckingham Palace, it wouldn't be high enough."

She passes remarks, we pass the De La War Pavilion at Bexhill on Sea
for the second time, having circumnavigated the whole British coastline.
Gallivant
Wandering about seeking pleasure and diversion.
Travelling with members of the opposite sex.

Andrew Kötting, second hand thinker

fig: 1996

Now painting in the sunshine.
The great out of doors.
Eden is busy articulating through signing her   *dreams.*

Today, she tells me of a dream in which a car breaks down and some dogs come out of the
forest to mend it. The faster they lick the car the quicker it goes. It spills into another story of a
family gathering at Christmas; Granny, Grandad and Big Granny are all there as is uncle Pig,
Joey, Billie, Etta, Mark and Tracey. We all pull crackers and inside the crackers, wrapped up in
coloured paper are whispers. And the whispers say things like:
Hello or I love you or Bugger.
Her imagination has found a higher ground.
Eden is eight years old.

Eden Kötting, 1996

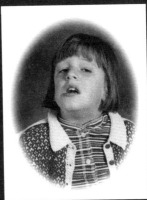

Eden school portrait, 1997

She will always be in my tiny little head.
Sempiternal
Feeling here, in this place my memory, solitary.
Having been with me,
constraining me,
full,
filling me, inspiring me.
Never momentarily, but lost like a trajectory, into the eversoBigbeyond..
Wassailing,
A surfing through this citylife underbelly,
Jostling with
and then bumping off (into), so many around me.
Comedown after the celebration; moribund, but a pickmeup could be waiting.
Always a possible, always visible,
but all this: (pin) pricked into insignificance
oooh the eversoBigbeyond.
I n q u i s i t i v e n e s s.
She takes another step forwards.
Me the Pollyanna in the face of the Jeremiahs.
Sounds of Locust and Ryoji Ikeda.
Mongrelising, adding, keeping and forgetting.
Working, feeding.
She and her more drawing; more than Haring.

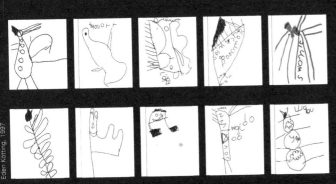

Eden Kötting, 1997

Donkeyhead

The branching roads of Eden's reveries; wherever they might be, but occasionally, apparently, she's far out on them.

Drifting by association and disparity.

Provoking a why?

Or what are we going to do tomorrow?

Or what did you have for food?

Or what did you have to drink?

Again and again she asks with her awful locution as a new world of communication and ideas opens up.

Eden and always the drawing.
France.

Sitting in the forest, lights off,

a place of solace,

safe from the bombard that has become this life.

Human genes likewise discard human bodies, moving on.

So I get up and go back to the house for supper.

Distant sounds of Denez Prigent, Bowery Electric and Jali Musa Jawara.

Proboscis and preparatory drawings for a map of perception, disseminated through libraries.

Later we will relight the fires.

Eden school portrait, 1998

Eden Kötting, 1998

In preparation for the SciArt year.

What's the name of that bloke I now know? Mark. Mark Lythgoe

You've turned me into this; this youandme this.

Thinking of her today as human model.

The littlun' sat nodding, minding her own business.

Me waiting for a heavy weight to fall.

Which is a problem.

Again the trouble with being born.

Eden school portrait, 1999

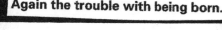

The more gifted a man is, the less progress he makes on the spiritual level.
Talent is an obstacle to the inner life

This my architecture of twaddle.
Then there's the SciArt phenomena, an adhocist debate.
The head swims in the wake of outbursts from others. All of this to now comprehend.
Landing in worlds Faberbookofsciencesque,

——————————————— Scientists. ———

Experts within facets of their chosen holes.
Dressed up and shouting at you in bloodstained I can'teverbewrong clothes.

Me

Head against the wall.
Undoing that which is riveted, embracing the contingent, whilst waiting for the clarification.
Devouring like a cultural omnivore, eating with the mouth open very wide, so as people might see inside.
Ideas jostling for a place to hide.
Now rooted in the notion of a pre intellectual, a subliminal self awareness.
An intuitive.

Sounds of Scorn, Philip Jeck, Iroy and Janek Schaefer.
Until then, after her birth I imagined myself capable of anything,
all the transgressions, all the adventures, always the dare. But now not.
Humility and old age have brought me here, via her.
Voyeur in the house of the devout believer and fundamental non questioner.

A recent quandary hit upon because of a big man with a guitar that frequented a working man's gym with me.

Pertaining to a modern as opposed to the postmodern but with hindsight, of **relevance** to the SciArt debate.
relevance to thingymajigs
form (conjunctive, closed) to antiform (disjunctive, open
purpose to play
design to chance
hierarchy to anarchy
mastery to knackered
artobjectprocess
footballsubuteo
distanceparticipation
creationlettingitallhangout
totalisationdeconstruction
thesisantithesis
presenceawaywiththefairies
centringdispersal
genretext

semanticsgibberish
robinreliantvauxhallcalibra
depthsurface
hollywoodpepysestate
interpretationagainstinterpretation
reading eyesclosed
signifiedsignifier
legiblescriptable
symptomdesire
johnbetjemanbarrybadblood
typemutant

phallicandrogynous
paranoiaschizophrenia
purposefuljourneygallivant
origindifference
metaphysicstakingthepiss
from determinancy to hither and dither.

And so to the proper nonsense.

4

More recent reflections on a state of mind.
Fig: 2000 a SciArt year.

Eden Kötting, 1999

A short history of decay
Phrenology and the art of propensities which is all right by me.
For the time being at least. Somewhat casually.
Mark and his department as the new phrenologists, determined that their discoveries,
(unlike Franz Galls), will stand the test of time. The reassuring and somewhat didactic findings, reminding
me of EM Cioran: *"I call simple minded any man who speaks of Truth with conviction; it is because he has
capital letters in reserve and employs them naively, without deception, without disdain".*

Postulating.
Thus the human intellect is unfit to study itself. This the multimedia show that is the mind.
E n t e r t a i n m e n t.
He likes these theories, taking other peoples theories taken from other peoples theories and theorising
his own theories. Postulating.
Not for the lab?
Antony van Leeuwenhoek the inventor of the microscope and
Kingdom Protista.

Lent Werner Herzog's Land of Silence and Darkness to Mark.
Phenomenal. An epic in all its understated hand fumbling glory.
Which brings to mind something that Herzog once said along the lines of

"Film is not the work of scholars but the Art of dimwits".
I find this reassuring, so I continue with
This my writing analogous to my thinking.
Mathematics as a short hand to logical problem solving.
A language seductive and accomplished and applicable, beautiful but somewhat incomprehensible.
So to metaphor; produced solely on the basis of a rich cultural framework, and an understanding or
at the very least a part understanding of this framework.
Falling, I fall overboard.
Fathomed and then forgotten.

Your mouth is open very wide, you should always put your hand in front lest people see inside.
We have our pictures taken by the fMRI scanner.
I slide inside the coil of a gigantic magnet.
Readings are taken from many angles and a computer translates the information into a three dimensional representation.
The pictures are very pretty, but the shape of my head is not.
This Filthy Earth.
In the Yorkshire Dales making a film, an Arthouse film.
Something for the scientist: Farmyard inspired theories may be too base and unsophisticated, too covered in the dung of their own origin to make sense but it is these theories I hang on to, and move forward with nevertheless. Science and its hard facts, but this my preferred speculation as philosophical dallyance? Nonsensicles.
Beginningtolookattheinnerself.
John Locke, (no relation to Sean Lock), and from the 17th century, (the European century of Beginningtolookattheinnerself), tells me:

"It is impossible for anyone to perceive without perceiving that he does perceive. When we see, hear, smell, taste, fear, meditate or will anything, we know that we do. This consciousness (which) always accompanies thinking is the Self."

Platitudinous.
We seem to have come a long way from Descartes' idea of the self.
To begin with him, (inside our heads, looking out on the world) and end up with Locke (not Sean), firmly on the outside looking in.
The thought passes as quickly as it is presented. But lingering; me now thinking about Eden's **sense of self.**
The brain too clever by half.
Her whole situation is a tyranny of subtlety, cerebrally and more over cerebellum ly.
Invalid and Faithofourtime
Each period intoxicated by an Absolute.
We cannot avoid being contemporaries: Me the Postpredicamentist ie. etc.
History as irony on the move.
Sounds of Pole, Warp, Low and Boards of Canada.
Minds jeer down on us, today this belief, tomorrow dead.
It all changes, those accepting it follow it in its defeat.

Then Bob's your uncle, along comes something else.

Perhaps the old belief might even be revived.

Demolished monuments reconstructed until they too fall over.

Francis Fukuyama's End of History and the Last Man.

It's a load of ludicrous.

Like car crashes, my mind thinks by accidents, the glory of a discomfort or the delirium of suffices. This my upstairs, a glory hole, in vain attempt to uncover the knowledgething.

The tickle of fancy.

Only left handed people are in their right minds.

Perception as to know or to understand, but still cofusionist whilst trying to.

A receptive process but for me just regurgitation.

In the name of **quest**. Inquisitive.

Deliberating but invariably forgetting. They tell me the processes that involve thinking, meaningful language, or problem solving are assigned to cognition, whilst those dealing with the non symbolic or concrete properties are identified as perception: size, colour, shape, texture and sound.

ie what colour is your hoover and what type of noise does it make?

Deadad.

Woke up, administered the morphine, dreaming, like **him** perhaps, but now holding on, worrying that I might have done my back in.

Then more lifting.

Carrying **his** carcass to the bathing room to be told by **him** about **his** dirty finger nails, the shampoo in **his** eyes and then the memories, as they do, flooding back about roles reversed: bathroom drawers, weights and measurements: now closed. **Deadad.**

Fig: 2001 a SciArt continuum.

So to more things that have cluttered up my existence.

Here we see:

My goal as an absence of goals.

Possibly due to a massive insult at the conceptual stage I've been left with no head control.

Athetoids in particular

And some harsh discoveries in the Wellcome Trust Libraries.

Hamburg: an art gallery: sat supposing once again.

Cause and effect as brilliantly portrayed in the work of Peter Fischl and David Weiss: *The way things go*

or

later tonight: Charlie Chaplin's ***Modern Times.***

A chaotic theory.

Eden has enabled me to accept the collapse of certainties.

She suggests the acceptance of the haphazard as the only probability.

In a world of jellyfish might Eden rule?

Zero G.
Star city and a model of the human brain with which to play keepy uppy.
Aptly named Arts Catalyst make it all possible for me to experience the brutality,
of a space with twice the gravity.
No need to elaborate, keep it nicely obfuscatory.
Sounds of Gurdjieff and de Hartmann.

Feet firmly on the ground.
I tried telling him that paintings and poems should be the fruit of pure psychic automatism, dictated by thought without any kind of control or reason.   (*Flipping heck* resounding around my head as I tell him this).
The scientist with a penchant for ladies, seductive in his foppish mancunian blather.

To what extent can the human brain be replaced by a collection of vacuum tubes and transistors?
Like the rat or monkey that cannot understand quantum mechanics so I/we am/are prohibited from
understanding certain aspects of existence, such as the relation between mind and matter.
Consciousness will always remain beyond my understanding.
Brain.

And yet it is one of the lightest organs in our bodies.
The skin weighs more and so does the yardage of intestine.
And all the questions that I still do not have the wit to ask.

A lesson in anatomy.
Rework Rembrandt's The Anatomy Lesson. Eden surrounded by every doctor that has ever had contact with her.
Mark and myself to find a place amongst the gathering.

My dysphoria increases daily.
I dally with the futility of my self inflicted lunacy and general skylarking.
What a laugh.
The idea that beneath this rational surface lies the naughty infantile other self, held in check by the cerebral
traffic wardens.Mess all this thinking, the brain's main function is to keep my organism alive and possibly
reproducing: partners permitting.

Frequency
Talking today with Toby, (consanguinity), and an aesthetic decision to try and originate as many sounds as
possible from those recorded inside the fMRI. The *Panasonic* type rhythms the *Ikeda* type frequencies,
wherever needbe, to possibly,
transpose them into the semblance of a melody.
In harmony.
Ambitiously and somewhat perversely. (For a brother in law).

Cerebellar executive functions.
Us moderns seek progress and subvert tradition ; then coming unstuck we seek solace in our folkloric heritage,
a berserk scramble to reconfigure something that was lost.

Singing Sands
To fill the Gallery with salt or the singing sands of Northumberland. They would emit an humanistic cry as you
walked upon them. As many grains as there are neuronal connections. But now after consultation with a power
that be we decide to lose, this our meta-for the billions of neurons sent shooting across the cortextial skies.
Pushing the brain piss up behind your eyes.

Empiricism
And a theory that the only theory is the theory of there being no theory. So let's get on with it.
He wants to be able to make sense and convey a semblance of sense from this the nonsense.
Through an exploration of the senses.

Sounds of Tosca, Tarwater and Zbigniew Preisner and People Like us.

Fig: 2002

Warning!

Beware the dangers of becoming intoxicated by symbolism.
Meaningless resemblance's, leading further and further away from the truth.
Swimming in bogus scientific language, regurgitated and half understood.

Muddleup
Science-Empirical, Art-Magical.
So what is science getting out of this symbiosis? keeps ringing in the head.
Peering through the net curtains at teenage spray can rebellion today and saw the creative
process as Iconoclast; a destroyer of religious images or concepts.

Psychogeographical muddleup.
Between hear and a seeing place.
Take the aphorisms and outbursts and structure them as if trawling my own particular landscape.
Pay attention to all of the details that have been touched and those that linger.
The second hand thinking and repetition should make their merry way through.
How far back to go? Where does it all start? To begin @ **fig: 1987** for instance?

Recumbent.

Face down, tongue out, moist duvet.
In her new blue and red and white stripy top.
Smelling nice, smelling cuddly, now fourteen, sad that there is so little interaction between her and the adults that fill her life.So full of expectation, but deflation when her attempts to make contact (via the holding hands or tickling face process), becomes nothing more than: *"Eden stop that now, leave Joey alone, John (the big bloke with the guitar from the gym) doesn't want to hold your hand all day."*

When it's fed it grows.
A seven year old girl with only half a brain has astonished doctors in Holland by becoming fluent in two languages, reports the Daily Telegraph. The child was diagnosed with a rare progressive brain disorder when she was three. To treat the condition surgeons had to remove the left hemisphere of the brain (which contains the speech centre) and fill the gap with marrow fluid. But when the girl was admitted to hospital earlier this year with tonsillitis, doctors discovered that she is now bilingual in Dutch and Turkish. "It was amazing" said Doctor Borstein. "I had to tell my students to forget all the neurophysiological theory they were learning. If this little girl could achieve so much with only half a brain, what could we not do with a complete one?"

Crick.

The astonishing hypothesis:

"your joys and your sorrows, your memories and your ambitions, your sense of

personal identity and free will are in fact no more than the behaviour of a vast assembly of nerve cells and

their associated molecules"

Ever alert.

In science there is no comfortable escape into the world of words.
No room for the Wittgensteinian jollyup.
But Richard Rorty reminds us to remain contingent, receptive to other vocabularies.
Metaphor as meta language not denoting but rather implying through resemblance.

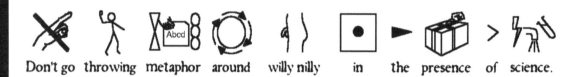

Don't go   throwing   metaphor   around   willy nilly   in   the   presence   of   science.

Metaphysics

and the some such not the **it** but **it's** behind you or there **it** goes or **it's** over there.

Our only hope is metaphor whilst dealing with this, the intellectual circus that performs inside the head.

Mayday.

The film now finished and infused with a rage still humming from This Filthy Earth and possibly
The Hoi Polloi. A film as first attempt at coming to terms with Eden's condition and my new state of mind.
A collaboration and the arcane nature of this my craft. (The Rosicrucianists spring to mind, again.)
Sounds of Hallucinator, Catpower, Johnny Cash and SubRosa.

Here   the   stored   images   of   past   experiences are   projected   into   the   future.

Children's shoes have far to go.

I see Mark and myself as the two children in the Startrite shoe advert.

We walked side by side along the road that is *the work*. Our goal was to explore the ridiculous notion of **Mapping Perception**, but en route we took each other to places that we had not been before.

To this end I would like to thank Giles Lane for bringing us together and shepherding us along the way.

I would also like to thank **Leila** for the company and her progeny without whom none of this would have been possible. She continues to take me there, as do my family.

New inmates with new enquiries will come to dig from within the confines of their own gulags, each of them a nissan hut of mistakes but always an attempt to undermine the perimeter fence.

Come by. There you have it.

To Eden, for when I'm gone.

Andrew Kotting
August 2002

Andrew Kötting, photograph of Startrite poster; Blackheath 2002

And of course: The Joubert Foundation for their Inspiration. **John Roseveare** and his ballooning. **John (poorcunt) Penfold and Loui** whose fire engine we borrowed. **Jeremy Pryce** @ Videosonics and his soundsof. **Alex Cromby Rodgers** for his fierce and slightly scarred intellect and **Tony Flemming** for helping him build. Kevin and his flock. **Sally** at the ICH and everybody else up there that knows me. **Russell and Jonny** for caring. **Ron Henocq** for making the last bit possible.

You sit at a piano for exactly four minutes and thirty three seconds no more and no less, and you don't actually do anything. Like Rauschenberg's white paintings, 'the canvas is never empty'. It's a glass of milk, you need the glass and you need the milk. Or you need the glass vial and, if you've got one handy, you need the last breath of a famous scientist. I know John Cage never wanted it to be but, to me, *4'33"* will always be sort of a favourite joke... well kind of a not funny one. He worked really hard to give the work the same rigorous structure as he did with his other pieces rigorously adding up the various sections to determine the precise length of the piece, etc. He demanded it be performed precisely. It's obviously a crucially important piece of music. The bit of this story that I really like though. It turns out years later that he made a mistake when he added up the time sections. So it became a lie to itself. And going back to Edison's last breath, I'd love to believe that it really was Edison's Last Breath but I'm certain that its a fake. It's too good to be true. I love it even more for that. There is nothing more beautiful than a beautiful lie.

About Art
I'm coming Marie... but I have to come slowly...
little pieces of me keep falling off.
Tales From The Crypt.

From time to time Marcel Duchamp taught in a Californian art college. It was at the time American macho abstraction painting was in ascendance. He walks up to this feverish slash and burn painter and asks "What are you doing?" The painter turns from his canvas and says, "I don't know what the mess I'm doing." As he walks away, Duchamp pats him on the back and says, "Keep up the good work."

It's a burger and fries. You need the burger and you need the fries. And you need the fat content, and you need the packaging, and you can't ever get one that is

About Mapping Perception –
Toby McMillan

Beware though the breathtakingly beautiful. For at any
moment. The telephone might ring. Or an aeroplane come
down in a vacant parking lot.
John Cage

About Lying
Someone once told me that Henry Ford, the car manufacturer, worshiped many 'great' people, none more so than Thomas Edison. He had collected many things that the scientist had owned or worked with. But his most treasured possession was a small sealed glass vial with a paper label hand marked 'Edison's Last Breath'. I thought that was great, I've always loved John Cage's piece of music *4'33"*, or the idea of it at least.

just 'small'. It's has to be a 'regular'. By the same token, I hope that most people, on some level, at least, when they do look at a totally white canvas, or listen to a silent piece of music, think to themselves "that's stupid".

About Eden
I've known her all her life. You may have heard Eden comes from the same gene pool as my children. My sister and Andrew had Eden. I have my kids with Andrew's sister. If you reduced Eden to maths she was a one in sixteen chance of being mine.

Like most children, she is very beautiful. Her world is a bit different from most. Too tall. Too short. Too left handed. Too much lying. Too fat. Too thin. Too poor and just too darn stupid.

About The Film
I wrote the music. I spent a lot of time getting rid of hiss and crackles and pops.
Then I got paid.
When you travel to Beirut. Don't be a Christian. Don't be a Moslem. Be a tourist.

About The Installation
You change the world by looking at it. If you stare at someone's back they'll turn around to look at you. There is no science or law that can explain it. But we all know it's true. They won't be able to stop themselves, even if they are a scientist. To me, that was the point to the installation sounds. We added room sounds, we added sounds of places a long way away, and aeroplanes and gravel paths, and we mixed them very low. Mostly because I have always loved that Perec spiel about jigsaws. The idea that every time you pick up a piece, think about it and put it back, every time you feel the bumps and the recesses, every time you try one piece against another, the jigsaw maker has already been there and walked before you.

New Orleans Diary – Andrew Kötting

June-July 2002

Convention
And so to New Orleans.
Voodoo, bayou and all things magical.
The Joubert Syndrome Convention.
In existence because of fierce determination.
People like Cheryl Duquette and Mary Van Damme, an intention,
and our journey made easier because of the support of The Gulbenkian Foundation,
Sian Ede, Leila
and my mother; Rita.
Dr Mark Lythgoe and Robyn come too.
Breakfast and a room full of *others*.
An impact on the senses never before experienced.
We all set about our *hellos* business and then to an air conditioned room where we sit and listen.
Cold on the inside hot on the out.
Stormy humid weather.
Some science in the auditorium with their *expert* backs to us.
We look at a rabbit with black and white stripes and they call it a zebra.
A mouse flayed right down to its dna.
Genetic engineering.
Brain deficits with defects in the genetic code.
Agenesis and maldevelment as middle of the road.
Negative projections and negative attributions to this the heavy load.
Consanguinity and the family tree.
Leesa and Toby, Leila and Me.
Here comes an oral motor intervention, there goes a systematic chromosomal instruction.
Everything working normally?
Dandy Walker and the art of being pissed.
The molar tooth sign and the infant deceased.
Mental confabulation, the mind meandering and then to the speech pathologist.
Watch her use her augmentative communication to help us realise a revelation.
I'm put in mind of cryptomumbojumboisms but words stick and the thrust is followed.
Neurological to neuropsychological,
Opthamalogical to neuro-opthamological,
Gait and balance to the radiological.
'*End stage renal failure*' and my ears prick up.

The cysts in her kidneys.
Precarious, the life that she lives.
The prognosis.
The outcome.
What *lies* ahead.
Some answers are hidden in that room somewhere.

Let's to work let's put some lipstick on the pig.
A physiological and morphological gad about.
A pleasure to be involved with this, the *diseased* community.
Her with her dancing eyes, me with mine.
So much to look at.
(The brain secretes thought as the liver secretes bile.)
Sat here thinking.
Then a day of tests for Eden to gauge where she might be at.
Visual perception and a book full of drawings:
Show me hydrant Eden, show me hydrant,
Show me stoop Eden, show me stoop,
 [the porch],
Show me closet Eden, show me closet,
 [the wardrobe],
Show me squash Eden, show me squash,
 [the vegetable],
Show me pollution Eden, show me pollution,
Show me infatuation Eden, show me infatuation, annihilation, regurgitation......
She hesitates, hovering, taking her time and then when the moment is right she points.
A mental age of somewhere between five and fourteen.

Here we see an evening:
Families from as far afield as the Australian outback or the sweet smelling Italian metropolis.
Banter around tables of Cajun scoff.
We connect with each other sharing the rub.
They're everywhere.
Meandering, sometimes bumping, bodies zig zagging.
Others perfectly *capable*.
William and Charles Hine looking drunk on their way to the bar but full of ***Eloquence***.
William tells of dreams he had as a kid; of being 'normal', dreading the wake up and the sadness
upon the realisation that he was as he is. In adulthood he yearns for those dreams again. Now 41 he
settles for his own website: **I'mme.com**.
Which moves and then settles me.

Finally

Solidarity with a sense of unity and familiarity, especially in the wake of the end of conference party.
Determined to write emotively about all the possibilities that is this the syndrome.
The *Other Sufferers* and their resemblance in serenity, delicacy and poignancy to all that is **Eden**.

Told today that he's not comfortable with the comfortable.
Never at ease with the normal.
This my abnormality.

Science as an air conditioned antidote to the warmth that might be superstition.

Notes for an Installation – Andrew Kötting

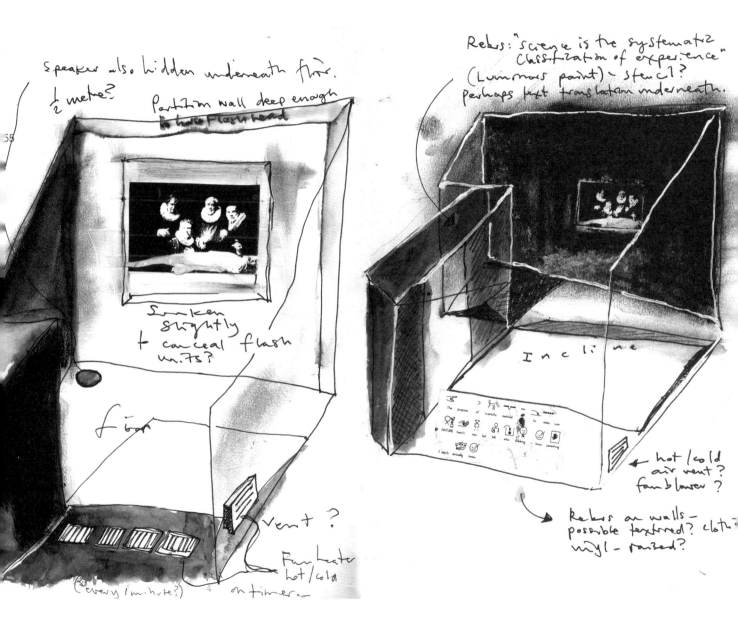

With the Installation we want to create an environment that talks about perception through the use of our main senses. We want the environment to be a contemplative space and through a process of immersion in this space we might be offered an insight into the world that is Eden's.

Mapping Perception as an Ontology or metaphysic.

The gallery as repository, a place of restriction and containment and paradoxically a place of transportation. The meaning of it is initially obscure but there should be a sense of order and theme to the pandemonium that is this place of reflection.

Another approximation.

We take Rembrandt van Rijn's *Anatomy Lesson* as springboard and catalyst. It is the backdrop and all seeing focus for our re enactment.

As testament to a spectacular body and confused conundrum that is her cognition.

A world re presented through her eyes.

She lies, stillbound, waiting for us to make sense of the carryon.

Movements of imperceptible clarity.

A meaning evoked through memory and icon.

A signifier and provocateur. We look towards a revelation and epiphany.

Timesgone.

We are impressed by the seventeenth century when the separation of the elements dilemma seemed barely to exist. Science and the Arts (philosophy in particular), formed a common endeavour and created a common body of knowledge.

A natural philosophy – the philosophy of nature.

There was a change. (In the West). The enquiry of the inner self began.

Samuel Pepys's Diaries (the estate on which Eden lives), Shakespeare's plays, (the Globe theatre, next to which her father writes this), or Rembrandt's self Portraits.

Dudley Sutton and Benji Ming are chosen for their striking resemblance to these timesgone.

Here we might also see

Rosicrucian philosophy.

It was disseminated throughout Northern Europe in the seventeenth century by an anonymous group of heretical writers. They promised religious and intellectual redemption to anyone who could decode their enigmatic signs.

Inquisition

We have slowed down the idea, we have almost stopped the inquisition, but ever alert to the deep heritage of scientific truths. A practical philosophy and series of judgments, revised without ceasing.

Tradition.

Our senses open to the zeitgeist, the bombardment of ideas set against the relics of past norms, surviving through a new digital mongrel tradition. This collaboration as pathetic attempt at new truths.

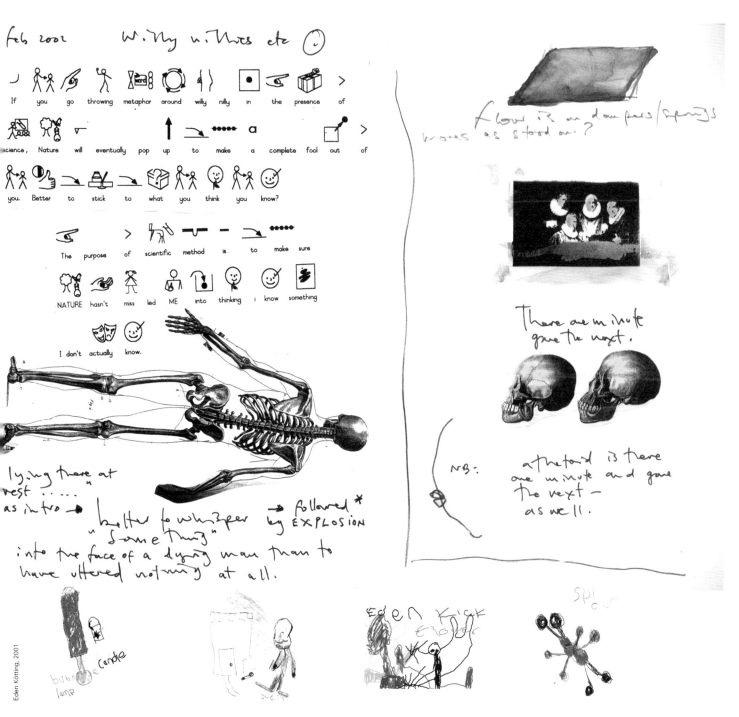

Feb 2002   W. Ny n. Thos etc

If you go throwing metaphor around willy nilly in the presence of

science, Nature will eventually pop up to make a complete fool out of

you. Better to stick to what you think you know?

The purpose of scientific method is to make sure

NATURE hasn't miss led ME into thinking i know something

I don't actually know.

lying there at
rest . . . . .
as intro →   bette to whisper   → followed *
              "something"   by EXPLOSION
into the face of a dying man than to
have uttered nothing at all.

flour is on dampers/springs
knows as stood on?

There are minute
gone the next.

NB: a thetad is there
       one minute and gone
       the next —
       as well.

bubo   e candle
lamp

Eden Kick
Enolosc

spi

Pepper's ghost illusion and
the implication of an image that is not there. Trickery.
A moment implied but tom fooled by the senses. If this could be achieved then we might well be barking up the right tree. Or do we hide the messages within the place into which we project? Luminous paint might do it in the wake of an en lightenment.

*The formation of hypotheses is the most mysterious of all the categories of scientific method. Where they come from nobody knows. A person is sitting somewhere minding his own business and suddenly – **flash!** – he understands something he didn't understand before.*
Robert M. Persig

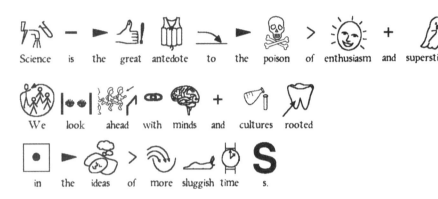

5

To apply our maxims to the surface itself.
In relief like the flocking on good restaurant walls.

Sounds of:
Entering the space as a place of sound. Sometimes cacophonous sometimes not around. Silent. Frequency gating and sine waving. The hush made audible. The sigh, high up or hidden under the ground. The whole working as an anthropological potion free to work its multifarious magic.

A stinker
Then there's the *smell of conception* as experienced through the odour of **88**. A rather expensive body cologne worn in the early hours of the morning of the thirteenth of June nineteen eighty seven, connected with the number 8 and all that that might connote symbolically or numerologically!

If someone had collected your shoes from the time you were a baby they might look something like this:
Eden's shoes can show the test of time.
Her toe and finger nails in a phial?
Artifacts pertaining to her long and precarious journey.

f loo

— or —

method

Kevin Belger
to Alex

[The Earl King
M. Zhel]

Tournier

...than Green
Words Apart ...
...various
...axims-
...phorisms
...s imposed

...tographic
...ints?

...ocking
...pliqué
...to on
...alls

Some rebus symbol
maxims/aphorisms
to hand ketracted onto
walls as a band
in room with
video?

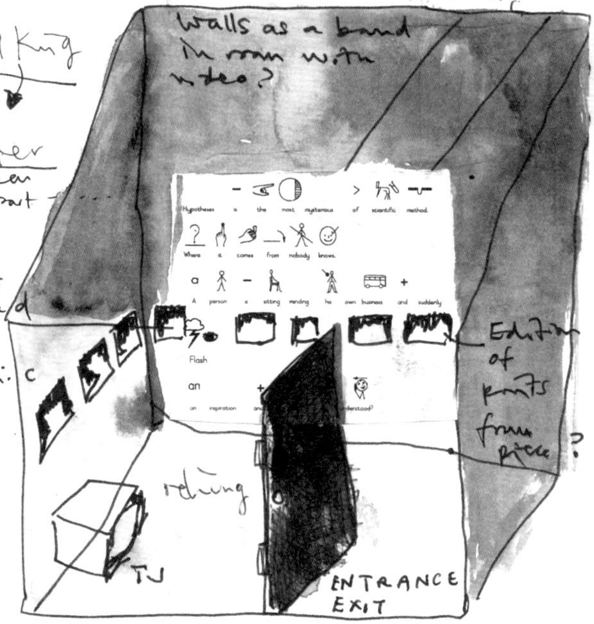

Hypothesis is the most mysterious of scientific method.

Where it comes from nobody knows.

A person is a strong minding his own business and suddenly

Flash

an

an inspiration and ... understood?

Edition
of
knits
from
piece ?

retiring

TV

ENTRANCE
EXIT

metallic type
notice board
(medical – lish)
with magnetic images
stick on.

"Science is the systematic
classification of experience"
⊙ or large?

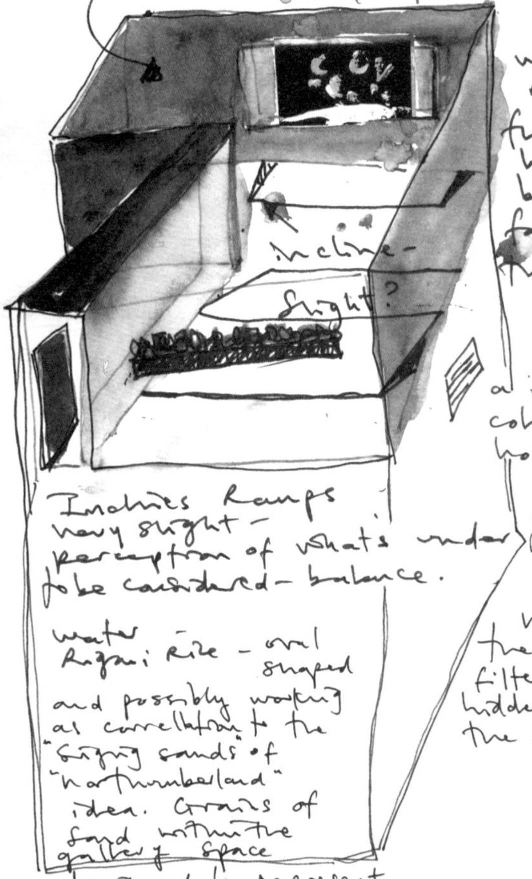

within
recess?
from lights
hidden
but
facing into
the gallery
?

Incline –
slight ?

a pocket of
cold air ?
hot air ?

Inclines Ramps
heavy slight –
perception of whats under foot
to be considered – balance.

noises from
the outside –
filtered / sampled
hidden within
the space.

water
Rising Rise – oval
shaped
and possibly working
as correlation to the
"singing sands of
Northumberland"
idea. Grains of
sand within the
gallery space
designed to represent
the number of nerve cells in the brain
i.e. 3 x the number of human brains
'living' in the world at this moment
in "THE MOMENT"

Andrew Kotting, installation notebook 2002

Notes for a Film – Andrew Kötting

The edit suite a room at Tall Stories, a G4 500.
It smells like a slipper in here.

The Script

Still evading the imposition of a finite meaning.

Disembodied voices.

Seen cinematically, these disjunctions might appear as affronts to narrative or as out to lunch avant garde collage.
Eden again our glue for the disparity.
Not against interpretation but never happy with the singularity of a reading.
Better a continuum, anti stuckist. The landscape over a picture of the landscape.
The topology rather than the *thing* in the gallery.

A bastard entity composed of a mish mash of other entities. Pick and mix.
This *our*

Circumstance of utterance.

Undecidable propositions as edit decisions now cajole for our attention.
Which bit goes where and why, become ineffable ponderables.
Mark now privvy to the process. If it fits leave it for the time being and a meaning might come along later.
Eden will act as the presenter and performer, (the mistress of ceremonies), giving us the potential for putting words into her mouth: (simulated) archive or the voice of pompous patronising authority.

Blindsight

Other empirical findings that have inspired such as blindsight, after patients sense of awareness has been damaged by some trauma or disease, but they are still able to catch a ball that they haven't seen. Things that aren't really there.

Hermann's Grid.

film stills

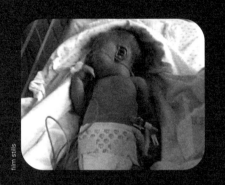

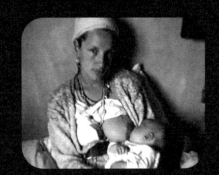

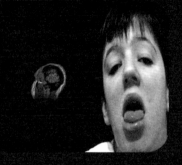

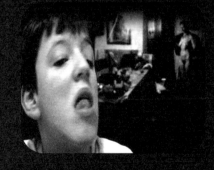

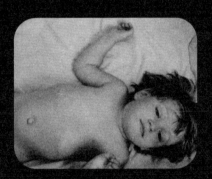

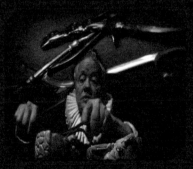

film stills

His teacher complains that he is backwards.

The film is the manifestation of the contemplation of fourteen years of Eden's life.

We distil the contents looking for an appropriation of what it was like.

Choice as the great eliminator.

There she is sitting on my lap and I drive her like a car.

To stimulate and cogitate that mind that is *her*.

Eye contact is hard but we see her laughing through sheer joy of the haptic, the sonic and the euphoric **experience.**

It will all find its own place in the film.

The use of blue screen chroma key to build up the layers to achieve the: *more than the sum of its parts.*

Mirrored.

The past with the present and now possibly her reflections upon a future.

The bits not always visible to the naked eye. The bits not *visible* at all.

This *our* experiment was not about *knowing* beforehand, moreover the enquiry, (as in *his* lab), was about testing the hypothesis in question: ie **Eden as our supposition, starting point and catalyst.**

The data produced has told us *something*. So we move forwards now approaching a full stop.

Finally

The distillation begins again and we look towards a concentration of ideas that might become **The Installation.** Refined, decanted and presented to be tasted. The ingredients of which have now blended.

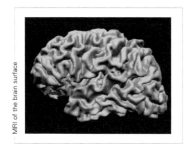

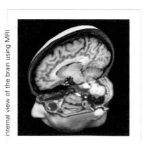

MRI of the brain surface

internal view of the brain using MRI

Something More – David G Gadian

Our understanding of how the brain works is being transformed by many new developments in science, not least of which is the emergence of increasingly powerful imaging technologies, including magnetic resonance imaging (MRI) (see David Thomas). These technologies enable us to visualise the various structures of the brain in remarkably fine detail, and to see which of these structures are activated on performance of particular tasks, such as moving the fingers or listing words beginning with 'c', or even just thinking about doing these things (see Chloe Hutton).

As a result, MRI has become a routine diagnostic tool in the clinic, aiding the diagnosis of brain disease, giving prognostic information, and also helping in the development and evaluation of new forms of treatment. And as a result, MRI is also extensively used in neuroscience research, with numerous scientific papers showing us which parts of the brain are activated when one feels elated, or angry, or scared, or whatever. How far can we go with this? MRI and other new technologies are certainly wonderful tools, and it is already evident that we can go a long way, a very long way. But can the scientific method really explain what love, or hatred, is, even if it tells us which parts of the brain are associated with these emotions? Can it really tell us what consciousness is? To look fully inside the brain, to really know what someone is feeling, maybe we need something more, and maybe a project such as *Mapping Perception* goes some way towards providing that something more.

David G Gadian is Professor of Biophysics and Head of Radiology and Physics at the Institute of Child Health and Great Ormond Street Hospital, University College London.

Eden aged 3

Eden aged 13

The Unlocked Door
Introduction – Mark Lythgoe

Last year a good friend Richard Gregory wrote a entertaining and inspiring editorial in the scientific journal Perception (Perception, 2001; 30: 1155-1156). This expressive piece describes the constraints of our perception and the effects of how we perceive our immediate environment, together with the delights of new discovery; all this was made possible though an account of an encounter with a locked door in the grounds of Cambridge University (an abbreviated account is below). This simple yet elegant article catalyzed a day long conversation between Andrew and myself about doors and how to open then. It was this conversation that led to the unusual design of the entrance and doorway to our installation. The door has been crafted to look and function as a normal door, yet it may appear locked and only opens in a way that we would not normally expect or perceive. The 'unlocked door' opens both the exhibition and the possibility to question our immediate surroundings within.

Eden at Louvre, September 2001

The Locked Door – Richard Gregory

Cambridge Colleges are far more than student halls of residence. Each has its own traditions, many from centuries of thoughts and jokes within their stone walls. It is a great privilege to live as a student in a Cambridge College, even more so to become a Fellow. Only Fellows are allowed to walk on the grass.

Ex-Fellows have dining rights for life and can stay in a grand guest room. As an Honorary Fellow I am allowed to stay in College for a few days at any time. Visiting Cambridge recently I arranged to stay in 'my' Colleges.

Instead of the usual guest room, in the main building, the college porter directed me to the nearby annex which I had never seen before.

The porter gave me two keys, attached to a large metal tag. The first key opened the outer gate. Steep stone steps led to massive double doors. These responded as expected to the second key. Inside the building was silent, as term had not yet started. Finding the guest room, I hurried to get ready for a dinner party in the town. So, I had to unlock the double doors from the inside.

There was a huge lock, with a tiny knob, quite a distance down, but no keyhole. I turned the little knob. Nothing happened. It rotated remarkably easily. Was it connected to the lock? Given its distance from the needed action, and its lack of resistance to turning, this seemed unlikely. So I looked for another mechanism – perhaps an electric switch, or a button? It was rather dark, but surely a switch or a button would be obvious? None was apparent.

Alone, in the almost dark and complete silence, as the seconds ticked away I confronted the situation. Looking more carefully in the gloom, I saw a surprisingly wide gap between the halves of the lock of the double door. Inside the gap, I could just see complicated metal fingers joining the doors. How did it open? Could this be a puzzle? Could it be a test for ex-members of the College? For Honorary Fellows, who might be past their ability to contribute to College life? Was I being tested by the Closed Doors?

Remembering the metal tag of the key ring, I took the keys out of my pocket, and inserted the end of the tag into the gap between the doors. Considering the anatomy of the metal fingers with care, I aimed the end of the tag at a couple of fingers, and pushed with some force. The fingers moved a little. The lock opened! So all was well.

Returning late in the evening, there was no problem. The key worked from the outside, as a key should. But when morning came – again I was confronted by the locked doors. Now there was more light, and I had the knowledge that the lock would open with a judicious push of the metal tag. But was this really the solution to the puzzle? Would the College impose such problem solving on its visiting Fellows? Surely not. This was hardly an appropriate academic challenge; though indeed it might be for a school of crooks, or prison officers. Wouldn't a number of Fellows be humiliated, locked absurdly in the College that is their mental nursery, their protection from incivilities of the world? Indeed, the grass is greener in a College.

In the morning light it was clear that there was no other mechanism. So it must be the knob. Of course it must. Turning it several times, and ignoring the sense that it moved so freely it seemed unconnected, apparently doing nothing – the metal fingers slowly parted. The doors opened.

The knob must have a lot of gearing, so rotating many times for a small movement it offered no appreciable resistance. This must be why it was so far away from the lock. This was the answer. How stupid not see it at once.

But I had discovered it was not the only answer. Perhaps no one else in the history of the College had discovered that from the inside the metal tag would open the doors. Intentionally or not, forty years after my College had awarded me a Fellowship, it gave me a curiously paradoxical lesson: that stupidity can make discoveries beyond intelligent scholarship. But was I worthy to walk on the grass?

Richard Gregory is Professor Emeritus of Experimental Psychology and Editor-in-Chief of the journal Perception at the University of Bristol.

Seeing oneself
Introduction – Mark Lythgoe

'Mirror mirror on the wall, who is the fairest of them all' – a childhood mantra that we have all chanted at some stage in our life. It is hard to escape reflections today, yet most of us still find time to court them to find out about our very self. But is it ourselves that we look at? This is a question that was raised by Richard Gregory in his editorial (Perception, 2001; 30: 903-904) that highlights the properties of mirrors and the implications for the way we see ourselves (an abbreviated account is below). In fact, as Richards explains, the majority of the time we never view our true image, that is, how others see us, as we mostly view a reflection of ourself. This of course creates the predicament, "what do I look like to others?"

Throughout the film making process, there was never an occasion that Eden wouldn't waddle through her home to sit in front of the video to look at herself after a day's filming. It was moments such as this, seeing Eden engrossed in the footage of herself singing, dancing or watching herself in the looking-glass, that we would wonder how she perceives herself. In the first half of the film we asked of one of her best friends, Billie, "And how do you think Eden sees the world?" after a moment of contemplation she breathes, "I don't know".

film still

Seeing oneself – Richard Gregory

There are puzzling phenomena of mirrors. Most discussed, is the right-left but not up-down reversal in a looking-glass. How can a symmetrical mirror reverse objects sideways yet not vertically? Surely a glass does not know its right and left. There have been a score of theories, invoking physiology, psychology, geometry, linguistics, and others.

What is the answer?
The mirror does not reverse the image. What is reversed is the object. For objects must be rotated, from direct view, to face the mirror behind them.

Small objects, such as books, are usually, because of gravity, around their vertical axis. If a book is rotated around its horizontal axis to face a mirror – it appears upside down and not right-left reversed. Writing on a transparent sheet, such as an overhead, can be seen a mirror with no reversal; because as it is not opaque it does not need to be rotated from direct view.

But what about a whole scene – such as in the driving mirror of a car? Why are the number plates of the cars behind reversed, right-left? The whole scene (or a room) cannot be rotated from direct view. But something is rotated – your head and your eyes. When you look in the mirror, your head is rotated 180 degrees from direct view of the scene behind. It is this rotation of the head and eyes that gives the reversal of the scene. Mirror-reversal is always given by object rotation; either of the objects seen, or the eyes that are doing the seeing.

One's face

One's own face is special. It is a unique mirror-object, as it is invisible to its owner without a mirror – so how do you know it is yourself? How does one recognise one's own face though never seen except in a mirror?

It may be that the related movements of the image to one's own movements is the initial key to self-identification. Would young children recognise themselves in a still photograph? Would time-delayed video allow self-recognition? I doubt it.

Well known experiments by Gordon Gallup, show that children below ten months of age do not recognise themselves in a mirror, and no animals except chimpanzees can do so. Gallup's experiment is to place a spot of rouge on one side of the face, and note whether the baby, or an animal, touches its own face or the mirror. Young babies, and animals except chimps, touch the mirror, not their face. Human adults, as well as chimps, touch the spot on the face. But is it possible that only humans and chimps are bright enough to relate self-movement, to movement of the mirror image, and deduce they are seeing themselves?

film still

film still

The Genetics of Joubert Syndrome – Craig L. Bennett, Melissa A. Parisi, Phillip F. Chance and Ian M. Glass

Joubert Syndrome (JS) is a rare, autosomal recessive genetic disorder, which means that both parents are carriers of the defective gene. Genetic testing is not currently available to detect this condition. Parents who have a child with Joubert Syndrome have a 1 in 4 chance of having another affected child in another pregnancy. It is estimated that 1 in 259 people are a carrier of the defective gene and roughly speaking, the frequency of the disorder itself may be 1 in 100 000 of the population.

JS is characterised by failed or disrupted development of the cerebellar vermis (see Byrony Whiting – The Cerebellum) and accompanying brainstem malformations. There is a distinctive magnetic resonance imaging (MRI) appearance in the brain termed the molar-tooth-sign that is of great diagnostic value but only recently recognised (see Kling Chong – Imaging Signs of Joubert Syndrome). Typically, a diagnosis of JS is made when this MRI finding is documented in an infant with hypotonia (a state of reduced tone in the muscles), episodic breathing disturbances and abnormal eye movements, along with a variety of distinctive facial and other features, including extra digits. Later, developmental delay and cerebellar ataxia (loss of the ability to coordinate muscular movement) usually develop. In some JS patients, visual defects are present in the form of retinal dystrophy (degenerative disease of the retina), coloboma (congenital anomaly in which a portion of the structure of the eye is lacking) and in others, renal abnormalities are present.

This disorder was first recognised in the 1960s by Dr. Marie Joubert. She observed that four siblings in a French Canadian family had disturbed neonatal respiration, abnormal eye movements, ataxia, mental retardation and most notably absence or incomplete development of the vermis, known as cerebellar vermal agenesis. Good estimates of the prevalence of Joubert syndrome have not been established, yet 350 families are registered from many parts of the world with the active family support group – The Joubert Syndrome Foundation (Columbia, MD, USA).

It has become apparent that the symptoms of JS patients vary widely and, variation within and between families greatly complicates genetic clinical studies. In addition, overlap with other cerebellar-retinal-renal disorders occurs and whether such disorders are located at the same position on the chromosome to JS genes is not yet known. Recently, the first Joubert gene locus was assigned to chromosome 9, by gene mapping two families of related parents in Oman. Interestingly, not all JS patients have the same defective chromosome 9. This finding establishes that more than one gene is responsible for JS, which confirms that genetic variability is present and therefore other JS genetic loci are yet to be discovered.

Research efforts to locate, isolate and determine the molecular basis of JS genes are difficult because of both the clinical variation and the genetic variability mentioned above. Several concurrent research approaches are ongoing and they include: (1) attempts to more stringently classify subtypes of JS; (2) detailed analysis of the natural history of this disorder; (3) mapping of genetic isolated families (e.g. French-Canadian, Jewish, etc.); and (4) genetic mapping of large families with several affected siblings. However, progress thus far, has been slow which is extremely frustrating to both researchers and families.

Unfortunately, no clear guidelines or health management recommendations specific to JS patients have yet emerged. This is because of the paucity of long term information, the difficulty in distinguishing between subgroups of Joubert, and in part because the diagnosis has only recently been made reliably, with the advent of accurate hindbrain MRI scanning. Currently, prenatal options are extremely limited for couples. Ideally, reliable DNA diagnosis of JS in an affected child would enable pregnancy predictions to be undertaken, if requested by parents, but as indicated above this prospect appears some way off. In addition, generating reliable fetal brain images of the cerebellar malformation sufficiently early in mid-gestation to be helpful remains problematic. Very unfortunately no curative treatment is available and it is hard to envisage such a scenario for some time even with gene discovery, because the malformations begin to occur very early in fetal life. Paradoxically, understanding the molecular basis of JS is the only means to generate specific and logical therapies to maximise the chances of affected individuals remaining in reasonable health and achieving their maximal potential in life.

Craig Bennett, Melissa Parisi, Phillip Chance and Ian Glass work in the Division of Genetics and Development, Children's Hospital and Regional Medical Center and Department of Pediatrics, University of Washington School of Medicine, Seattle, Washington.

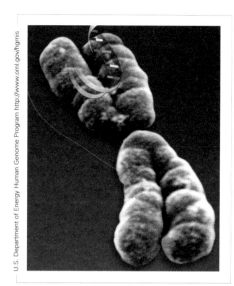

U.S. Department of Energy Human Genome Program http://www.ornl.gov/hgmis

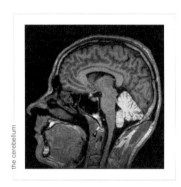

the cerebellum

The Cerebellum: the little brain – Bryony Whiting

The area of the brain called the cerebellum is one of the most important and impressive parts of the human brain. It is situated underneath the rest of the brain, tucked in behind the top of the spinal cord (the brain stem) and is the first port of call for much of the information on physical equilibrium coming into the brain from the rest of the body. The first anatomical descriptions of the cerebellum (also called the parencephalon or epenkranis by early scientists) were made by Aristotle nearly two and a half thousand years ago; although he misinterpreted the brain to be a secondary organ that served as a cooling agent for the heart. Despite this early work, however, it wasn't until 400 years later that researchers like Galen started to actively investigate the cerebellum. Even then progress was slow. The first detailed descriptions of the structure of the cerebellum were not made until the end of the eighteenth century when Malacarne, an Italian anatomist and surgeon, made careful dissections of the cerebellum. He named different areas of the cerebellum after common objects of which he was reminded and some of his terms, for example the vermis (worm), the lingula (tongue) and the flocculus (flakes), are still in use today.

The name cerebellum literally means 'little brain' and it is so called because it looks just like a miniature version of the whole brain. Like the whole brain, the cerebellum is made up of two halves (hemispheres) that are joined together by a middle section (called the vermis in the cerebellum or the corpus callosum in the whole brain) and both the cerebellum and the whole brain have a tightly convoluted outer layer.

The main function of the cerebellum is the co-ordination of movements. This involves combining incoming information from other areas of the brain and spinal cord with sensory information from muscles at the same time as controlling and monitoring motor output. In addition to these motor functions, the cerebellum has also been argued to be involved in memory, emotion and even language. There is, however, much controversy over these possibilities and researchers are still, and will be for the foreseeable future, trying to discover exactly what the functions of the cerebellum might be.

Bryony Whiting is a Cognitive Neuropsychologist in the Developmental Cognitive Neuroscience Unit, at the Institute of Child Health, University College London.

Magnetic Resonance Imaging (MRI): How To Look Inside the Human Body – David Thomas

At the centre of every hydrogen atom in every water molecule in the human body, there lies a tiny magnet. In everyday life, since these small magnets are weak and relatively very far apart, they are unaware of each other's presence and point randomly in all directions. However, when the body is placed in the strong magnetic field of an MRI scanner (where the magnetic field is about 30,000 times stronger than the Earth's natural magnetic field), these tiny magnets line up with the strong field, in the same way as iron filings orientate themselves when placed around a bar magnet. When this alignment occurs, the body becomes temporarily magnetised, and this magnetisation can be used to generate the signal which makes an MR image.

If you push a compass needle away from North, as soon as you let go it will swing back to its original orientation. A similar situation exists for the magnetisation of the human body when it is lying in an MRI scanner. However, rather than using a physical push to misalign the magnetisation, a short burst of radio waves is used. This works because the tiny magnets in the water molecules in the body are all spinning at a certain 'resonant' frequency of around 100 MHz, i.e. in the radio frequency region of the electromagnetic spectrum. Applying a burst of radio waves at this frequency while someone is inside the MR scanner causes an electromagnetic force to push the body's magnetisation out of alignment with the scanner's magnetic field. Like the compass needle, this is an unnatural state for the body's magnetisation, and so it quickly returns back to its original position. As it does so, it sends out radio waves at the resonant frequency, and these are detected and form the signal that makes the MR image. Importantly, the amplitude of the radio waves emitted by a water molecule is crucially dependant on its particular environment, and it is this dependence that allows us to distinguish different types of tissue and creates the striking contrast observed in MR images. Small variations in the scanner's magnetic field allow the frequency of the signal to be dependent on exactly where it has originated from, and in this way two or three-dimensional images of the body can be created.

David Thomas is an MRI Physicist in the Wellcome Trust High Field MR Research Laboratory, Department of Medical Physics, University College London.

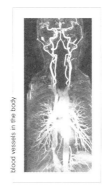

blood vessels in the body

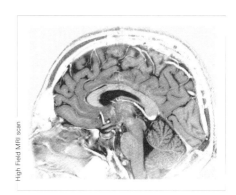

High Field MRI scan

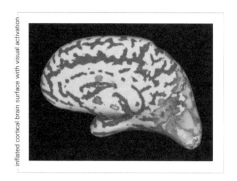

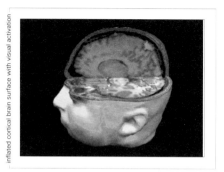

Images of the Mind – Chloe Hutton

Brain activity can be imaged using a technique called functional magnetic resonance imaging (fMRI). MRI in general allows detailed volumetric images of structures within the body to be acquired safely and non-invasively (see David Thomas). With fMRI, the person in the MRI scanner performs a task and the related brain activity can be detected. This is possible, thanks to the physiology of brain function and the physics of MRI. When we think, the area of the brain that is working needs more oxygen, so the blood supply increases to provide it. The change in the amount of blood oxygenation causes an increase in the MRI signal intensity where the brain is thinking (coloured area) in the functional MRI image. By acquiring a series of images over time, a picture can be constructed of the activated regions of the brain.

fMRI can therefore be used to detect the specific regions of the brain that are involved in performing specific tasks. For example, the part of the brain involved in seeing, known as the visual cortex, can be detected by showing a person pictures while they are being scanned. A series of images of the brain are acquired where each whole brain image may take a few seconds to acquire. Usually a few hundred or more images are acquired during the task. Each image represents a snapshot of the brain at the corresponding moment. A statistical analysis of the fMRI images results in a picture of the activity in the brain corresponding to seeing (as illustrated above).

With fMRI it is possible to see the regions of the brain involved in the primary senses such as seeing, hearing, smelling, tasting and touching. It is also possible to detect brain activations involved in tasks such as mental arithmetic, reading or memory and even higher human brain functions involving emotion or abstract thought. Using fMRI, functional maps of the human brain can be constructed, which further our knowledge about the brain and provide additional insight into the workings of human mind.

Chloe Hutton is Research Fellow in MR Image Processing in the Wellcome Department of Imaging Neuroscience, Institute of Neurology, University College London.

Imaging Signs of Joubert Syndrome
– Kling Chong

Children presenting with the Joubert Syndrome often have some characteristic appearances on their brain scans. The diagnosis can be made using Magnetic Resonance Imaging (MRI) or Computed Tomography of the brain. The main finding is that of an absent or extremely small cerebellar vermis (see Byrony Whiting).

This is best seen on coronal (vertical) or transaxial (horizontal) images of the cerebellum. On these images, the cerebellar hemispheres appear to be separated from each other by a cleft of cerebrospinal fluid (this is fluid which circulates around the brain, spinal cord and through the ventricles of the brain, and helps to protect the brain against injury). On closer inspection, a rudimentary vermis may be seen in the upper part of the cerebellum. Associated with this abnormality is a distortion of the shape of the brachium conjunctivum (superior cerebellar peduncles), which connects the cerebellum with the midbrain.

These tracts contain efferent fibres and thus mostly bring information out of the cerebellum. Lesions in this tract result in a disorder of coordinated movement. On transaxial images at the level of the midbrain, this sometimes gives the appearance of the profile of a molar tooth and some authors have described it as 'the molar tooth sign'. The rest of the brain usually appears structurally normal.

Kling Chong is a Consultant Neuroradiologist in the Department of Radiology at the Great Ormond Street Hospital, University College London.

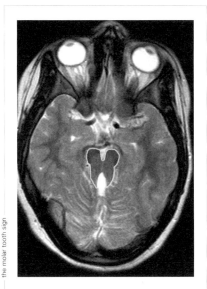

the molar tooth sign

Unlocking the Doors of Perception – Richard Gregory

In *An Essay Concerning Human Understanding* (1690), John Locke (1632-1704) founded British Empiricism. He is described by Bertrand Russell as "the most fortunate of all philosophers":

Not only Locke's valid opinions, but even his errors were useful in practice. Take, for example, his doctrine as to primary and secondary qualities. The primary qualities are defined as those that are inseparable from body, and are enumerated as solidity, extension, figure, motion or rest, and number. The secondary qualities are all the rest: colours, sounds, smells, etc. The primary qualities, he maintains, are actually in bodies; the secondary qualities, on the contrary, are only in the percipient. Without the eye, there would be no colours; without the ear, no sounds, and so on.
A History of Western Philosophy (1946)

Russell thinks that there are good grounds for secondary qualities. But, as Berkeley pointed out, the same arguments apply to primary qualities. So: "Ever since Berkeley, Locke's dualism on this point has been philosophically out of date." Russell goes on to say:

Nevertheless, it dominated practical physics until the age of quantum mechanics in our own time. Not only was it assumed, tacitly or explicitly, by physicists but it proved fruitful as a source of many very important discoveries. The theory that the physical world consists only of matter in motion was the basis of the accepted theories of sound, heat, light, and electricity. Pragmatically, the theory was useful, however mistaken it may have been theoretically. This is typical of Locke's doctrines.

It is tantalising that Russell does not go on to say just why this dualism is mistaken. Evidently he accepts differences between appearance and reality (as for jaundice and so on), so where is Locke's error? Is the answer to be found in Berkeley's writings?

George Berkeley (1685-1753) denied the existence of matter apart from perception. Then he cheated with God, by saying (in the words of Ronald Knox) that "when there's no one about in the quod, the tree will continue to be, since observed by yours faithfully, God". As Berkeley became a Bishop, this might have seemed a strong defence; for the rest of us, it is not. For surely one might ask: Who observes God – to make Him exist? If the observer is not necessary for God's existence, why should observing be necessary for matter to exist? If we criticise Locke for a too-passive theory of perception – the blank slate and all that – we may explode in amazement at Berkeley's view that perception is so active it creates matter.

Berkeley argues his celebrated case in the *Dialogues* (1713), with two disputants: Hylas (scientifically educated common sense) and Philonous (Berkeley himself). Hylas asks rhetorically: Can anything be more repugnant to common sense, than to believe that there is no such thing as matter? Philonous replies that he does not deny the existence of sensible things – that are perceived immediately by the senses – but that we do not see the cause of colours or hear the cause of sounds. Both agree (as Russell says) that, "the senses make no inferences". Isn't this the key point (apart from God) where we may disagree with Berkeley? We might say that Locke's general account is too passive – not allowing perceptual inference. Once this is accepted, Berkeley's account of perception as effectively creating matter is unnecessarily active. Hence in my view, the intellectual sense of calling perceptions hypotheses.

Objects may be suggested by sensory data, but can be far richer, and can exist though not observed. On this account, object-perceptions are created by brains as predictive hypotheses of what might be out there. The idea that private hypotheses refer to public realities is too active for Locke and not daring enough for

Berkeley, but this does not mean it is wrong. Wittgenstein looks at these issues in terms of his 'language games'. Writing of private experience he says,

The essential thing about private experience is really not that each person possesses his own exemplar, but that nobody knows whether other people also have this or something else. The assumption would thus be possible – though unverifiable – that one section of mankind had one sensation of red and another section another.
Philosophical Investigations (1953)

Wittgenstein points out that 'red' has two uses – private and public – which really needs two words. He invites us to look at the sky:

Look at the blue of the sky and say to yourself: `How blue the sky is! When you do it spontaneously – without philosophical intentions – the idea never crosses your mind that this impression of colour belongs only to you. ... And if you point to anything as you say the words you point at the sky. I am saying: you have not the feeling of pointing into yourself, which often accompanies 'naming the sensation' when one is thinking about 'private language'."

Wittgenstein then says, subtly: "Nor do you think that really you ought not to point to the colour with your hand, but with your attention." He then invites the reader to think about "pointing to something with the attention". Wittgenstein then asks: "But how is it possible for us to be tempted to think that we use a word to mean at one time the colour known to everyone – and at another the 'visual impression' which I am getting now?"

His answer is: we don't turn the same kind of attention on in the two cases.

Wittgenstein does believe in an 'inner' and an 'outer' world; for he had just written: "Now, what about the language that describes my inner experiences and which only I myself can understand? How do I use words to stand for my sensation?" He leads us to rules of this language game, and to behavioural concomitants of, for example, pain. Here I for one get somewhat lost. One accepts that a friend is seeing the blue sky though he is not pointing upwards, and that he is in pain though he makes no movement or sound. Why, indeed, can't one say that another's sensations are hypotheses for us, much as external objects are hypotheses? That is, they are not sensed at all directly; but there is indirect evidence for public objects and for another's sensations. Of course there is no certainty in either case. But why should certainty be expected?

Philosophers would have benefited by thinking more about illusions! Why do we, with Locke, tend to say that primary qualities are in objects while secondary qualities are in us as observers? If we are seeing, say, a bicycle wheel, its apparent circularity corresponds to its smooth running. So appearance fits object reality. (Though of course it may appear as an ellipse, if presented at any angle other than normal. We make mental adjustments as well as perceptual shape constancy, to maintain harmony of object reality with appearance.) But when we see the sky as blue, there is no at all obvious physical thing, or object, 'behind' the colour causing it. When we realise that the colour is due to Raleigh's selective scattering of light, we are provided with a physical causal explanation – somewhat equivalent to the bicycle. But rightly or wrongly (at least for non-physicists) the scattering is hardly recognised as an object corresponding to the appearance. In both cases, however, we can make predictions to experience from physical knowledge, and from physical knowledge to experience. This is so whenever we recognise a cause of an appearance, which may, however, require technical understanding. Then, surely the primary/secondary dualism starts to disappear. Indeed, doesn't it simply go away?

Does this unlocke the doors of perception?

An Index of Participants

Alice Angus is Co-director of Proboscis and a curator and writer. She assisted with the project management of *Mapping Perception* and edited the CD-ROM.

Craig Bennett, Melissa Parisi, Phillip Chance and Ian Glass work in the Division of Genetics and Development, Children's Hospital and Regional Medical Center and Department of Pediatrics, University of Washington School of Medicine, Seattle, Washington.

Kling Chong is a Consultant Neuroradiologist in the Department of Radiology at the Great Ormond Street Hospital, University College London.

David G Gadian is Professor of Biophysics and Head of Radiology and Physics at the Institute of Child Health and Great Ormond Street Hospital, University College London.

Richard Gregory is Professor Emeritus of Experimental Psychology and Editor-in-Chief of the journal Perception at the University of Bristol.

Chloe Hutton is Research Fellow in MR Image Processing in the Wellcome Department of Imaging Neuroscience, Institute of Neurology, University College London.

Katrina Jungnickel is a freelance cultural researcher for arts and business projects. She co-edited the *Mapping Perception* book with Giles Lane.

Andrew Kötting is an artist and filmmaker, the director of the numerous shorts and the acclaimed first feature *Gallivant* (1996). His second feature, *This Filthy Earth*, was premiered at the Edinburgh International Film Festival in August 2001. The film won the Best Use of Digital FX prize at Hamburg International Film Festival. Andrew's short films include: *Donkey Head, Hoi Polloi, Hubbub in the Boababs, Smart Alek, Klipperty Klopp, Anvil Head the Hun, Acumen, Self-Heal, La Bas and Kingdom Protista.*

Billie Macloed Kötting is Eden's cousin.

Eden Kötting was the star of *Gallivant* and the inspiration for *Mapping Perception*. Eden suffers from a rare neurological condition known as Joubert Syndrome in which a small part of the lower portion of the brain (the cerebellum) is underdeveloped. This causes Eden to have a variety of symptoms including trouble with her speech, motor co-ordination, eye movements and breathing.

Giles Lane is founder and Co-director of Proboscis. Giles commissioned both Andrew and Mark to create projects for COIL journal of the moving image and later brought them together to work on *Mapping Perception*. In addition to his work for Proboscis, Giles is Visiting Research Associate to MEDIA@LSE at the London School of Economics and was a Research Fellow at the Royal College of Art between 1998 and 2002.

7

Janna Levin is a Cosmologist at the Department of Applied Mathematics and Theoretical Physics at the University of Cambridge.

Mark Lythgoe is a Neurophysiologist based at the Institute of Child Health and Great Ormond Street Hospital where he uses Magnetic Resonance Imaging (MRI) techniques for investigating brain function and developing possible therapies for children suffering from stroke. Interested in the public understanding of science, Mark has contributed to the new Birmingham Discovery Centre with *Brain Tuner*, an interactive installation in which one can investigate the brain areas that control our senses. Over the past 8 years, Mark has collaborated with a wide variety of artists – one of his first projects, working with Helen Sear in 1995, investigated the place of medical imagery in art and culminated as a publication in COIL journal of the moving image. In 1999 the joint exhibition *Chimera* with visual artist Jayne Gouge utilised the technology of MRI to create an unusual bridge between what we see and the way we see it. More recently Mark has worked with Annie Cattrell, producing sculptures of our thoughts from functional MRI brain scans, which were exhibited in Spring 2001 at the Anne Faggionato Gallery, London. Mark has been chosen to present the 2002 prestigious Dorothy Hodgkin Award Lecture by the BA (British Association for the Advancement of Science) on *Mapping Perception.*

Leila McMillan is Eden's mother and partner of Andrew. She appears throughout the *Mapping Perception* film and installation. She also created the digital animations and costumes for the film.

Toby McMillan is the sound designer for both the film and the installation parts of *Mapping Perception*. Toby has been a professional musician as well as studying Film & Time Based Media and working in the film industry. Co-incidentally he is Andrew's brother-in-law, being married to Andrew's sister at the same time as being brother of Andrew's partner Leila.

Benji Ming is an ex-punk, 'performance' artist, mountaineer and historian who has worked with Andrew on various projects. Benji has some French and a little German but is perhaps best remembered for 'his men in pants routine'.

Dudley Sutton is a well-known actor who has appeared in many films and on television since the 1960s. He recently appeared in Andrew's feature film, *This Filthy Earth*. Other credits include Ken Russell's *The Devils,* and Derek Jarman's *Edward II.*

David Thomas is an MRI Physicist in the Wellcome Trust High Field MR Research Laboratory, Department of Medical Physics, University College London.

Bryony Whiting is a Cognitive Neuropsychologist in the Developmental Cognitive Neuroscience Unit, at the Institute of Child Health, University College London.

Acknowledgements

Mapping Perception is a Proboscis project
Collaborators Andrew Kötting, Giles Lane & Dr Mark Lythgoe with Eden Kötting
Assistant Project Manager Alice Angus
Book Co-Editor Katrina Jungnickel
Marketing & PR Catherine Williams

Funded by Sciart Consortium (Production Award Winner, 2000), Film Council
(National Lottery award), London Production Fund, Calouste Gulbenkian Foundation
& South East Arts

Supported by Royal College of Surgeons' Unit of Biophysics at the Institute of Child Health,
Great Ormond Street Hospital, Royal College of Art & Kent Institute of Art and Design, Maidstone

Film Credits
A Film by Andrew Kötting, Mark Lythgoe et al
Produced by Giles Lane
Sound and music by Toby McMillan
Online editing Remote Films: Russell Stopford & Jonny Stopford
Technical support Stephen Connolly, Berkley Cole and Nick Gordon Smith
With Eden Kötting, Dudley Sutton, Benji Ming, Leila McMillan, Andrew Kötting,
Mark Lythgoe and Billie Macloed Kotting
Additional Camera Gary Parker
Tele Cine The Lux and Todd Ao
Animations Leila McMillan

Installation Credits
An Installation by Andrew Kötting, Mark Lythgoe et al
Curated by Giles Lane
Sound Design by Toby McMillan
Online editing Remote Films: Russell Stopford and Jonny Stopford
With Eden Kötting, Dudley Sutton, Benji Ming, Leila McMillan, Andrew Kötting,
Mark Lythgoe and Billie Macloed Kotting
Construction Alex Cromby Rodgers and Tony Flemming
For Cafe Gallery Projects Ron Henocq, Director & Malcolm Jones, PR